Heart of Wisdom, Mind of Calm

*Guided Meditations to Deepen
Your Spiritual Practice*

CHRISTINA FELDMAN

Element
An Imprint of HarperCollinsPublishers
77–85 Fulham Palace Road
Hammersmith, London W6 8JB

The website address is: www.thorsonselement.com

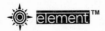

and *Element* are trademarks of
HarperCollins*Publishers* Limited

Published by Element 2005

Christina Feldman asserts the moral right to
be identified as the author of this work

A catalogue record for this book
is available from the British Library

ISBN 0 00 717524 8

Printed and bound in Great Britain by
Creative Design and Print (Wales), Ebbw Vale

Contents

Introduction

*W*e all long to be happy and free from the struggles and conflicts that scar our lives. We search for ways to find a heart of wisdom and a mind of calm. We yearn to be a conscious participant in creating a world for ourselves and others imbued with peace and understanding. Throughout our lives we do all that we can to bring an end to feelings of alienation, estrangement, and suffering, and to forge relationships of intimacy and warmth. Meditation is intended to transform us, to show us the way to free ourselves from the grip of fear, division, and confusion. The practice of meditation illuminates our life, inwardly and outwardly, showing us the path to freedom and wakefulness.

Meditation is not a means of fleeing from life, nor is it a quick-fix solution to all of the difficulties and challenges we may meet. But it is a path that teaches us to be increasingly present, honest, and awake in each moment of our lives. It is a direct means of healing the estrangement and division that too often separate us from others and ourselves.

Depth of wisdom, compassion, and peace are not sought in transcendent experience, nor projected into the future, but are nurtured within this heart, mind, body, and life in the present.

For thousands of years people have retreated to the solitude and stillness of deserts, mountain tops, and monasteries seeking an inner renewal, depth, and authenticity. But the great teachers of the past and present who truly inspire our own journeys do so not solely because of some dramatic spiritual breakthrough experienced in solitude, but through their commitment and capacity to embody their wisdom and depth of compassion in every area of their lives.

Initially, when we face the struggles, challenges, and conflicts that are part of living, we react with the belief that they are obstacles to be overcome or subdued. When we meet the swirls of confusion that can cloud our own minds or the emotional storms that shatter our hearts, we are prone to believe that they are wrong or a personal imperfection. But through our own experience in meeting the difficult and challenging, we come to understand that resistance, blame, judgment, or suppression do little to bring about healing and the end of sorrow. A path of meditation, directed towards the release of our hearts and minds, encourages us to turn our attention directly towards the places of challenge and difficulty we are most prone to flee from or abandon. This is where the seeds of peace and understanding plant their roots.

Meditation encourages us to step out of the pathways of blame, judgment, and rejection, and ask ourselves where healing begins in this moment. The end of sorrow, we begin to understand, does not rely upon eradicating everything unpleasant or challenging in our lives—that is an impossible task. The end of sorrow and struggle is born of our capacity to make peace with all things and to hold the events of our life in a heart of loving kindness and understanding.

Meditation is a path of awakening, an inner journey of direct experience. It has a direction and clear sense of aspiration—serenity, balance, open-heartedness, compassion, and deep inner wisdom all lie at the heart of meditative teachings and paths. Equally, meditation is a path of embodiment, teaching us to approach all of the events, people, circumstances, and moments in our lives with profound integrity, loving kindness, and equanimity. Meditation is not a journey of self-improvement—it is dedicated to the relief of anguish and struggle wherever they appear. Meditation is greater and vaster than just a technique or formula for living—it is the cultivation of a heart of wisdom and mind of calm.

Genuine meditation is no stranger to any of us. Long before we undertake a formal meditation practice we have all encountered glimpses of profound peace, compassion, and serenity, moments of deep inner stillness, times of genuine connectedness with nature, other people and ourselves. There have been times when the busyness of our minds has calmed and we have found ourselves listening, seeing, and responding with a natural sensitivity and patient intimacy. We have all met moments when our hearts have opened and we have found ourselves able to receive the sorrow and distress of someone we care for, or even a person we don't know, without fear and with a natural compassion. We have all experienced times when we have felt truly at ease within our own bodies, minds, and lives.

Too often these moments of depth and stillness feel like random occurrences. We are inspired and touched by them and yet they feel so fleeting and are too often inaccessible to us. Meditation practice teaches a way of being present and awake at all times, to ourselves and to the world, a way of resting in inner stillness, receptivity, and understanding.

Meditation is a path of cultivation and a discipline born of dedication to peace and depth. Patient intimacy lies at its heart. It is also a path of the present. None of us can alter or recover a past that has already gone by; the future is yet to come and we cannot guarantee how it will unfold. The moment we are in is the only moment that can be lived fully and in which we can find transformation. Meditation encourages us to turn directly towards our lives and this moment. They are the grist for awakening. It is not a quest to find a perfect moment, but a way of cultivating balance, sensitivity, and clarity within all the joys and sorrows of our lives. We come to understand that the source of genuine happiness, joy, and peace lies within our own hearts and minds, and not within the changing events of our life. Meditation is not a denial of past or future, but an understanding that we are writing the history of all the future moments in our lives through the way in which we attend to and live the moment we are in.

Too often we live in a fog of confusion and busyness, governed by impulse, habit, and reactivity. We find ourselves frantically trying to do more and more each day, torn between the multiplicity of demands that compete for our attention. Our lives can be filled with lost moments—interactions, conversations, sounds, sights, and feelings that we have neglected to attend to. Leaning into the future or floundering in thoughts of the past, we lose the richness and simplicity available to us in the present. Meditation practice is a direct way of reclaiming those lost moments—the life we can miss through neglect, inattention, and busyness.

Our meditation practice begins right where we are, in the life we are living, with our willingness to take the first steps of being attentive and present. There are a vast variety of spiritual paths, lineages, and traditions available to us. They vary in their styles, yet they share an emphasis on integrity, commitment, serenity, and wisdom. All meditative paths serve to nourish our hearts and minds, inviting us to explore the possibility of great depth, authenticity, and compassion in our lives. We nurture, through meditation practice, a climate of heart, an inner culture that is receptive to deep understanding and transformation. We learn to shed the layers of confusion and agitation that too easily cloud our capacity to live with great sensitivity.

Meditation is an art, and like any other art it asks for both dedication and discipline. At the heart of every meditative path is a dedication to peace, compassion, authenticity, and freedom. Genuine discipline is not a tyrannical code governing our actions and life, but is born of our dedication to all that is truly liberating and healing. The styles, practices, and techniques of meditation are the container or discipline in which we bring to fulfillment the peace and freedom we deeply treasure.

There are two dimensions to meditation: one is the form and the other is the spirit. They are interwoven and indivisible. Meditation is much more than becoming proficient in a particular technique. The techniques of practice are ways to articulate and cultivate the spirit of awakening. It is equally true to say that the paths and the goals of meditation cannot be separated. If we aspire to peace, understanding, sensitivity, and compassion, then we are also asked to practice meditation in their spirit. If our meditation practice is to lead to an open heart, clear mind, and greater loving kindness in every area of our lives, then it asks us to cultivate those qualities in every step of our path. Patience and dedication are key elements in the deepening of meditation.

Creating a Meditative Setting

Initially as you begin to practice developing attention it is worthwhile to create an environment around you that is supportive. A corner of your bedroom or any space in your home that is simple and quiet will serve. Find a chair or cushion that you can return to and as far as possible create in that space a meditative environment.

Dedicate a period of time each day to spend in formal meditation. There is no prescribed right amount of time; however long you are able to give to your meditation practice is worthwhile. Don't expect that every time you sit down to meditate you are going to have amazing breakthroughs, peak experiences, or moments of great rapture. What you meet in your meditation is the mind and heart you bring to it. Sometimes you will be sitting with a mind of chaos, filled with the plans or memories of your day. What is valuable is making the effort to be aware of that mind, however it is. The moments of stillness you commit to each day are always worthy moments. They are times of cultivating calm attention, awareness, and sensitivity that will begin to impact upon every area of your life.

When you sit down to meditate, ensure that you turn off your telephone, radio, and television. Allow yourself to unhook for a time and care for the quality of your own heart and mind. Increasingly we feel compelled to be perpetually available and engaged. Times of meditation are times to be engaged with stillness, appointments we make with ourselves.

It is often helpful to dedicate a period of time at the beginning and the end of the day to be wholeheartedly committed to cultivating our meditation practice. The effects of these times of stillness and focus will increasingly begin to pervade all of our day. We will come to see that calm attention, peace, sensitivity, and open-heartedness are not random experiences or accidents we occasionally encounter in life. They live within our own hearts and minds, born of awareness and wise attention.

There is no right posture to meditate in—you can use a chair, bench, or cushion—but find a posture that is upright and alert. In your meditation posture you are embodying the qualities of heart and mind you are seeking to develop. Within that uprightness, also find a deep sense of ease and relaxation. Battling with bodily discomfort in meditation is not conducive to finding the well-being and sensitivity we are seeking to nurture. If your body is particularly exhausted or distressed, it is even fine to lie down to meditate, although in this posture you may need to make a resolved commitment to be awake and present. The posture to seek for is the posture that allows you to be at home and at ease within your body.

Approach your meditation times as times of dedication. Commit yourself to being as fully present as it is possible for you to be. As you begin to practice, clarify your sense of intention. Take a few moments to reflect upon what this meditation is in the service of, what this time is dedicated to. The meditation is in the service of peace, calm, and sensitivity. Dedicate yourself to being attentive, clear, and focused. Let go of all preoccupations with the past and future. This is not a time for planning and rehearsing the future, nor for recycling thoughts about the past. Beginning your meditation with a clear sense of intention is an encouragement to establish yourself in the present. Meditation is a time of caring for your well-being and cultivating serenity and depth.

Meditation can introduce us to moments of great joy and opening. It will also make us increasingly aware of the places where we react most habitually and close down most persistently. Through sustained and dedicated practice we learn to embrace the difficult and the delightful, the joyful and the sorrowful with the same welcome, interest, and inner balance. In essence meditation teaches us to be awake and present in the midst of all things. This is the home of genuine understanding and depth.

CHAPTER I

Cultivating Attention

*A*ttention is the key that opens the door to inner peace and awareness. Learning to bring a loving and mindful attention to all the moments of our lives, we find ease everywhere. Without attention we live only on the surface of life. The song of a bird, the beauty of a sunset, the cries of someone who needs us are lost to us. It is only when we are attentive that we are able to explore our inner landscape and learn the lessons we are asked to learn if we are to live with authenticity and freedom. To be touched by anything in the world, to love and to live fully, we need to be present and awake. If we are to live with compassion, balance, and generosity, we need to cultivate the art of attentiveness.

Wise attention is a means of simplifying our inner landscape. Observing our own minds, we see that they seem to be filled with a cascade of thoughts, obsessions, memories, and preoccupations. We can feel overwhelmed by the fragmented thoughts and images that saturate our consciousness, a casualty of the busyness of our own minds. Attention teaches us to calm this busyness and agitation. Learning to be attentive, one moment at a time, is learning to rest in a deep sense of inner ease.

The art of clear, focused attentiveness is finding calmness in the midst of agitation, serenity in the midst of chaos, simplicity in the midst of complexity. We do not need to flee the world to discover this profound inner calm; we do need to learn how to release ourselves from fragmentation and distractedness.

Interest is the primary building block of wise attention. Wherever there is interest in our lives, energy and attention naturally follow. Wise attention is founded upon our interest in being free of confusion and fragmentation. It grows in the heartfelt interest we bring to understanding what it means to live a life of peace, calmness, and understanding.

Attention is the common thread that runs through every meditative discipline and art. It enables us to cut through the habits of entanglement and speculative thought and the reactions that trigger agitation. Through calm and gentle attention we learn to cultivate the clarity and sensitivity that allow understanding and stillness to deepen. Wise attention is a gesture of kindness to ourselves, freeing us from the chaos and abrasiveness of a mind that is too easily scattered and divided.

Attention is cultivated through learning to focus upon one object, one moment at a time. Learning to attend wholeheartedly to that object, we illuminate it, forming a bond of connection. It becomes our anchor in the present moment. Whenever our attention drifts away, we learn to come back, renewing our connection with that anchor.

Cultivating attention requires great patience, for we are sometimes swimming against the habits of a lifetime of being distracted and entangled. Yet attention is not born of willpower or control, but a calm commitment to being present and awake. In the practice of developing attention we need to bring a deep sense of ease and relaxation, yet also to balance that ease with a committed perseverance and dedication.

It is important that meditation does not become yet another task to add to a list of things we must do. It should be approached as a time of deep ease, a time of reconnecting with our capacity to rest with calmness and wakefulness in all the moments of our lives.

The attention we develop in meditation practice will begin to make an impact on our lives. As our inner busyness begins to calm, we will be more aware of the nature of our minds and bodies. We will find that we are less prone to being governed by impulse and reactivity. Our capacity to be more present with all things will be enhanced and we will discover a refuge of serenity and balance within our own hearts and minds.

Attention is the art of cultivating happiness and well-being. We do not need to postpone that ease to a time in our lives when there are fewer demands upon our attention. We can discover it now—in the midst of a life of activity, a mind that has thoughts and a world that is ceaselessly bombarding us with a multiplicity of impressions and demands. Attention awakens us—to ourselves and to everything that comes into our world.

There are a variety of ways of learning to develop attention and calm in our lives. Spending some time on a daily basis in formal meditation cultivating a focused and single-pointed attention will make a significant impact upon the quality of our lives, and learning to bring that wise attention to all the contacts and interactions we engage in daily will deepen and enhance our capacity to live with spaciousness and calm.

Attention in itself is not difficult; it is remembering to be attentive that is challenging. But in discovering that wise attention is the source of deep inner happiness and well-being, our dedication to its cultivation will grow.

Mindfulness of Breathing

When you sit down to meditate there are times when you find yourself sitting with a mind that is overfull with thought, distraction, and busyness. Your first reaction to this may be to feel that this is the wrong time for you to meditate. In reality, the times of agitation in our lives are the times that most urgently invite us to cultivate calm and simplicity. Finding it difficult to be with ourselves and to explore our inner landscape is a cue that signals the urgent need to find a sanctuary of inner calm.

It is helpful to cease thinking of agitation or turmoil as an insurmountable obstacle to mediation and to developing serenity. The obstacle lies not in the agitation and chaos, but more often in our resistance to these states.

Accepting that our minds and hearts are chaotic, confused, and overfull is the first step in developing calm. Dismissal and judgment only add a further layer of tension to the turmoil already present. Acceptance is the beginning of the transformation we seek. The next step is to approach that chaos with a calm and gentle attentiveness. It is just one moment at a time we are asked to care for and make peace with. Discovering our capacity to nurture even a little serenity and attention in the midst of chaos will deeply enhance our confidence in ourselves and rescue us from foundering in agitation.

GUIDED MEDITATION:
MINDFULNESS OF BREATHING

Find a posture that is as relaxed and comfortable as possible.

Gently close your eyes.

From the top of your head to the tips of your toes, gently and systematically move your attention down through the whole of your body.

As you do so, consciously relax any part of your body that is registering tension or agitation. Soften any knots of tightness that you become aware of. Pay particular attention to your face, shoulders, and hands, allowing them to soften and relax.

Let your hands rest on your legs or rest together lightly. Focus your attention for a few moments on the palms of your hands, being aware of whatever sensations are present.

Let your body relax into a sense of ease, consciously being still in your posture.

Gently bring your attention to rest within your breathing. Be aware of the whole movement of your breath from its beginning to its ending. Be aware of the expanding and relaxing of your chest and abdomen with each breath.

Now make your breath slightly deeper and fuller, sensing the movement of the in-breath as it moves into your abdomen. Don't exaggerate the movement of your breath too much, just deepen it slightly.

Bring your attention to the movement of your out-breath. Follow your outgoing breath to its very end, sensing when it has fully left your body.

With each breath you take, give particular attention to the out-breath, to the release of your breath and your body relaxing. Sense yourself breathing out tension and agitation.

When your mind is agitated, thoughts will clamor for your attention. Each time your attention is drawn into the thoughts or images that appear, just notice them, not pushing them away but also not becoming lost within them. Give them the barest of attention, acknowledging them but knowing that this is the time for cultivating stillness and calmness.

Gently bring your attention back to be fully aware of the next out-breath. Breathe out the agitation.

You may notice that the pressing thought patterns have an impact on your body, making it feel restless. If this happens, just consciously recommit yourself to being still and relaxed within your body.

Continue focusing upon your breathing, keeping it just slightly fuller and deeper than it would normally be.

Let yourself be fully present within each out-breath, staying with it until the beginning of the next in-breath.

Notice the slight pause between the ending of one out-breath and the beginning of the next in-breath. Let yourself rest calmly within that pause.

Sense the beginning of the next breath and your body's response.

When you are ready, open your eyes and come out of the posture.

Counting and Naming

When our minds are dominated by thought, our breathing is almost invisible to us. The force and compelling nature of the images and thoughts swirling through our minds drown our capacity to find an oasis of stillness within ourselves. At these times we can learn to highlight our breathing through counting or naming our breath. The counting or naming is a means of bringing us closer to the moment-to-moment experience of our breath, thereby establishing a greater sense of connection with the moment we are living. Naming or counting just one breath at a time allows us to step out of the cascade of thinking that sabotages clarity and simplicity.

When using counting or naming it is important that it does not become mechanical or habitual, but that each time we use a number or word, it is directly connected with our breathing at that moment.

Through the simple practice of counting or naming we learn to cultivate a clear sense of focus and one-pointed attention. It is not a means of suppressing thought, but a way of slowing down the momentum of thinking, enabling us to see the movements of our minds more clearly. Learning to befriend our breathing, to forge a bond of simple intimacy within this most natural process, is a means of learning to cultivate that same simple intimacy with our minds.

GUIDED MEDITATION:
COUNTING AND NAMING

Let your body settle into a posture of ease and balance.

Take a few moments to be aware of your body, letting your shoulders, face, neck, and hands soften and relax.

Let your eyes gently close.

Sense the place where your body contacts the ground, chair or cushion. Be aware of the sensations that are present in those points of contact.

Breathe a few slightly fuller breaths, consciously establishing your attention within your breathing.

Let your breathing find its natural rhythm and depth.

With the in-breath count one, with the out-breath two. With the next in-breath three and the out-breath four.

Continue counting with each breath until you reach ten and then begin again.

Ensure that your counting and your breathing are harmonized and co-ordinated.

Let the pressing thoughts in your mind simply rest in the background, appearing and fading away just as the sounds and bodily sensations present in that moment also appear and fade away.

There may be times when your attention becomes lost in thought and you lose track of your counting. Don't be judgmental in these moments. The moment you are aware of being lost, just begin again with the counting, starting at one with your next in-breath.

Don't be hurried in your counting, simply be present with one breath at a time.

NAMING

Instead of counting you might find it useful to use a few simple words as an aid to cultivating a more deeply focused attention.

Again, rest your body in a posture of alertness and calmness, and gently close your eyes.

Bring your attention to your breath moving in your body. Let your breathing be relaxed and natural in its rhythm.

As you breathe in, use a simple phrase: "Breathing in calmness." As you breathe out, use the phrase: "Breathing out, letting go."

Let the phrases just rest gently in your attention. Apply them to each in-breath and each out-breath.

As you use them, sense their meaning and their possibility in that moment.

Feel free to experiment to find the words or phrases that feel meaningful to you and relevant to your state of mind.

Try not to be overly elaborate with the words you use. Keep them simple and allow them to suggest the quality of heart and mind you feel is most needed.

Let your attention rest within the phrase and your breath simultaneously. Allow the phrase to bring you increasingly close to your actual experience of breathing.

There may be many moments when your attention moves away from your breathing and into a thought or bodily sensation or sound. Don't resist those movements, simply notice where your attention is and then gently return to the next breath.

As you return your attention to your breathing, even if you have been lost in thought for a considerable time, begin again with a sense of patience and the clear intention to be present.

You may find you are aware of only one or two breaths before your mind begins to wander or be attracted to an appearing thought. This is fine—here too you learn to cultivate clarity and sensitivity. What is significant in the meditation is the quality of attention, simplicity, and sensitivity you are cultivating moment to moment. Being attentive to your breathing is a powerful reminder to be present in a wakeful and sensitive way.

When you are ready, open your eyes and come out of the posture.

Rising and Falling

GUIDED MEDITATION:
RISING AND FALLING

Take a few moments to relax into an upright and alert posture.

Let your eyes close gently and your whole body soften and relax.

For a few moments take a few slightly fuller breaths, paying particular attention to your outgoing breath and releasing it fully.

Let your breathing relax and find its own natural rhythm.

Bring your attention to rest in your abdomen, noticing how your abdomen responds to each inhalation and each exhalation.

Sense the rising and falling of your abdomen with each breath.

With each movement of your abdomen make a quiet mental note to mark what is happening.

Note "rising" with the in-breath and "falling" with the out-breath.

Ensure that the mental noting is directly linked to what is actually occurring in your abdomen.

Let your attention rest within the noting and the movement in your body simultaneously—rising, falling, rising, falling.

Sometimes you may find it helpful to place your hands gently over your abdomen as you are practicing. This will enable you to feel more fully connected with the movement of rising and falling as it happens moment to moment.

At times your attention will move away, into past, future, images, sensations. As far as possible just notice those departures and note where your attention has gone with simplicity and calmness.

Return your attention to your abdomen, once more noticing the rising and falling in your abdomen with each breath.

Sense your breathing calming and focusing your attention.

Sense yourself letting go of busyness and agitation, moment to moment.

When you are ready, open your eyes and come out of the posture.

Breathing with Visualization

The keys to developing sustained and clear attentiveness are patience and consistency. Meditation is called "practice" for obvious reasons—we are learning not to subdue or suppress our minds and hearts, but to train them. We are training them in the pathways of calm, serenity, balance, and simplicity. It is a training in kindness for ourselves, a way of cultivating an inner climate of openness, receptivity, and clarity. Patient intimacy is the secret to developing any form of meditation.

GUIDED MEDITATION:
BREATHING WITH VISUALIZATION

Settle your body into a relaxed, upright posture of calmness.

Allow your eyes to gently close.

Take a few moments to be aware of the stillness of your body and its contact with the ground, cushion, or chair.

Bring your attention to rest within your breathing. Establish your attention in your body, breath, and the moment.

Consciously let go of thoughts of past and future.

For a few moments follow the whole movement of your breath from its beginning to its ending, being fully present in its natural rhythm.

Sense your breath as a stream of light entering and filling your body.

As you breathe out, sense yourself breathing out that stream of light.

As your breath fills your body, sense it bringing brightness and spaciousness.

Allow your attention to be fully focused on breathing in light and breathing out light.

With each breath, sense a deepening of inner spaciousness and calm, a release of any agitation that may be present in your mind or body.

For as long as possible, keep your attention on the image of breathing in light and breathing out light.

Memories, thoughts, images and sensations will continue to arise. Sense the possibility of allowing them to pass without becoming entangled in their contents.

> Allow your attention to be fully absorbed by your breathing.
>
> Let the spaciousness that begins to emerge pervade all of your mind and body, calming any waves of restlessness or unease that may be present.
>
> When you are ready, open your eyes and come out of the posture.

One-Pointed Attentiveness: The Concentrated Mind

When your attention is more focused and concentrated, your breathing will become lighter and shallower. The movement of your chest and abdomen in response to your breathing will become almost imperceptible. If this occurs, do not try to force a deeper breathing.

You may notice that as your breathing becomes more imperceptible, your body also begins to feel lighter and more spacious. Thoughts and images will continue to appear, but you can sense a calming of all of the activities of your mind. The thoughts that appear will cease to clamor for your attention, arising and yet also passing much more quickly. Your attention will feel more effortless and joyful.

To further deepen the attention, it is helpful to make its focus even simpler.

GUIDED MEDITATION:
THE CONCENTRATED MIND

Find a posture for your body that is as balanced and relaxed as possible.

Gently close your eyes.

Take a few moments just to be aware of your body, bringing your attention to all the places where your body makes contact with the ground, cushion, or chair.

Just be aware of the sensations at those points of contact—warmth, pressure...

Bring your attention to your breath just at the point where it enters and leaves your body.

Focus your attention calmly yet fully on the area of your upper lip and nostrils.

As your breath enters your body, just be aware of the sensations that arise—the coolness of your breath, tingling, whatever sensations appear in the area of your upper lip and nostrils.

Sustain your attention in that area, with whatever sensations are present, until you sense the touch of the out-breath at your upper lip and nostrils as your breath leaves your body.

Be aware of the warmth of your out-breath as it leaves your body.

Let your attention rest clearly and gently in the area of your upper lip and nostrils.

You might find that your breath becomes almost imperceptible. If this occurs, let whatever sensations are present at your upper lip and nostrils be the focus of your attention. Don't try to make your breathing fuller or deeper, just let the sensations of the breath entering and leaving be the point where your attention rests.

You may be aware of thoughts arising, but notice that few of them linger or have the power to draw your attention away from your selected focus.

Bodily sensations may also arise, but as your concentration deepens you may notice a perceptible change in your sense of your body. A very deep sense of bodily ease and relaxation may appear as your concentration becomes more established. You may notice that the boundaries of your body begin to blur and the sense of solidity in your body softens. This is fine. Just continue to keep your attention focused on the area of your upper lip and nostrils.

If there are moments when your attention is drawn to a thought or bodily sensation, just notice this and gently return to focus once more on the area of your upper lip and nostrils.

As you focus on this area, notice how the sensations change, at times becoming very subtle.

Sense the ease and simplicity that come with deepening attention. Let yourself rest within that ease.

As your concentration deepens further, notice the deeper calmness and spaciousness that begin to pervade your body and mind.

Rest with ease within that calmness, allowing it to deepen from moment to moment.

When you are ready, open your eyes and come out of the posture.

Listening

Every day of our lives we are exposed to the world of sound. Some of the sounds that come to us we welcome and delight in—the song of a bird, the laugh of a child, a favorite piece of music. These are the sounds we wish to prolong, sustain, or have more of. Then there is a spectrum of sound we greet with less than delight—the traffic outside our window, the non-stop ringing of telephones in our workplace, the voice of someone we dislike. These are the sounds we want to end, to get rid of, and find ourselves resisting. The sounds we deem as unpleasant we translate as being noise and they trigger aversion or feelings of being invaded inwardly.

As long as we live in this world of sound there will be count-less moments when we will be unable to control the sounds we receive—the pleasant, the unpleasant, and the neutral will always be part of our world. To try to control them makes us defensive and contracted, living with avoidance and the fear of being over-whelmed. Meditation practice embraces the world of sound and our capacity to attend to it with spaciousness and sensitivity. We begin to understand that sound holds no intrinsic power to obstruct calmness and inner stillness.

Listening with Sensitivity

Listening meditation is a direct way of learning to befriend and find space within the world of sound. In meditation we learn to let go of our judgments of noise and attend wholeheartedly to the spectrum of sound that will continue to be part of our lives. It is a powerful way of cultivating sensitivity and attention.

Learning to listen with sensitivity and calm attention, we learn to be present with all of the sounds that come to us, excluding none. We learn to open to the world around us, understanding that sound is the sound of life. We cultivate a receptivity that is firmly grounded in balance and simplicity, and discover the possibility of not being lost or overwhelmed by any of the sounds that come to us. Rather than putting in earplugs to block out the sounds of the world, we turn directly towards them with our attention. We discover our capacity to be present and awake within the spectrum of sounds that arise, we see their endings, and we explore the space between sounds.

Genuine calmness cannot rely upon blocking out any dimension of our world. It rests upon our willingness to embrace every facet of life. Listening with mindfulness, we discover the inner ease and calm available to us in all the moments of our lives.

At times when our inner world feels particularly contracted, our minds overflowing with thought, or our hearts burdened with difficult emotions, learning to listen with sensitivity and attention is a powerful means of cultivating a greater inner spaciousness and calm. There can be moments when it is simply too difficult or demanding to connect with the turmoil of our hearts and minds. Wise effort and wise attention in those moments involves taking our attention away from the inner intensity and finding a place of connection and attention that offers some ease and simplicity. The glimmers of calm and spaciousness we can find within listening are the qualities we can bring to being present, in a more spacious and balanced way, with the waves of turmoil within ourselves. So learning to listen with sensitivity softens the feelings of being imprisoned in turmoil and allows us to see more clearly and deeply.

GUIDED MEDITATION:
LISTENING WITH SENSITIVITY

Take a few moments to settle into a posture of alertness and calmness.

Gently close your eyes and fully relax and soften your body. Bring your attention to any area of your body that feels tight or contracted. Let your shoulders, hands, and face soften and relax.

Bring your attention just to listening. Try not to look for sound; simply be attentive to the sounds that are present in the moment.

Settle your attention into a receptive listening.

Notice the sounds that are near and those that are more distant.

Sense, if you can, the beginnings and the endings of the sounds.

In sounds that are constant, sense the differing tones and intensities within the apparent constancy.

Notice what happens in your mind or emotions in relationship to the sounds you are receiving.

Be attentive to how quickly the mind brings judgments or labels to the sounds.

Simply sense the moments when your attention has shifted from just listening into the judgments, descriptions, or associations that have arisen in your mind.

See if it is possible for you to let go of the world of interpretation and come back to just listening.

Notice the moments when you find yourself leaning towards the sounds you enjoy or contracting in the face of sounds you find disturbing.

Explore whether it is possible for you to sustain your attention in just listening, embracing the pleasant and unpleasant equally, bringing an equal sensitivity and receptivity to both.

When thoughts arise, allow them to pass, letting them just be whispers in the background of your attention.

Stay as fully present as possible with just listening.

Sense the arising and passing of sound, the beginnings and endings of the sounds that come to you.

Notice the moments of stillness and silence that may be present in the interlude between the ending of one sound and the beginning of another.

Sense the moments when you find yourself listening to silence.

In the times of silence, don't leap to find another sound to attend to, but rest within the silence.

As your attention deepens, so does your capacity to listen. You may begin to find yourself aware of subtler levels of sound coming from the world around you and the world within you.

You may begin to hear the sound of your heartbeat or your pulse.

Attend wholeheartedly to whatever sounds appear, relaxing in the silence that emerges in the absence of sound.

Sense the spaciousness and calmness that begin to emerge with your deepening capacity to just listen with sensitivity and simplicity.

Simply be present in the presence of sound, in the presence of silence.

When you are ready, open your eyes and come out of the posture.

Listening to Life

Listening with sensitivity and spaciousness is a practice not only reserved for times of formal meditation. We can learn to listen with calmness and simplicity in the midst of all of the situations in our lives where we feel bombarded or overwhelmed by a multiplicity of sounds. Learning the art of listening with wise attention, we discover the possibility of moving through a world of sound, fully engaged and yet never lost.

Sound is always available to us as an object of attention in our lives. Instead of feeling that the sounds in our world undermine our well-being and calm, we can learn to utilize them as vehicles to deepening sensitivity and inner stillness.

GUIDED MEDITATION:
LISTENING TO LIFE

As you move through your day, experiment with bringing your wholehearted attention to listening.

You might do this when you are walking down a busy street. Listen fully to the different sounds and tones that come to you as you would listen to the different instruments in an orchestra.

Sense the sounds that are deep, those that are shrill, those that are repetitive and those that are just whispers in the background.

Notice the judgments, concepts, or feelings that arise in you in response to the sounds.

Explore whether it is possible to let go of all of the associations and overlay of concepts and return your attention to just listening.

Sense, if you can, the beginnings of sounds, how long they last as predominant impressions in your consciousness and when they begin to fade away and to be replaced by new sounds.

Let your attention be rooted in the receiving of the sounds, sensitive to their changing nature. If there are times of silence, no matter how brief, let your attention rest fully in that silence, receptive to stillness.

Explore how spacious and open it is possible for you to be, receiving sound without being overwhelmed.

There are many times in the day when you can explore this practice, utilizing the sounds of the world as a focus for attention and the ground upon which you develop sensitivity. Sitting in a restaurant filled with sound, traveling on a train or in your car, working in a busy office, experiment with taking a few moments just to listen fully, not rejecting any of the sounds that come to you but nurturing your capacity for receptivity, attention, and calmness within them.

If you discover moments in your day when you find yourself resisting the multiplicity of sounds that come, labeling them as noise and flinching or closing down before them, approach them as invitations to cultivate balance and openness.

Explore whether it is possible to turn your attention directly towards the sounds you find yourself trying to shut out.

Sense what happens as you engage with those sounds with a willing and conscious attention, noticing the changes within them, their beginnings and endings.

Sense whether it is possible to find within yourself the calmness and steadiness born of conscious engagement.

Establish your attention in your capacity to listen with sensitivity rather than being preoccupied with whatever it is you are listening to.

Moment to moment, cultivate the capacity to find wholehearted attention and calm wherever you are.

Calming the Mind

Visualization can be another effective means of cultivating calmness and simplicity. We can gather and focus our attention upon a visual object, simultaneously calming and releasing much of the fragmentation and scatteredness that can pervade our minds and bodies. Attentiveness is always a twofold process: cultivation and letting go. We cultivate a calm and clear one-pointedness; we let go of distractedness and agitation.

With visualization we learn to bring mindfulness, interest, and clear attention to the object we have chosen. We learn to be intimate with it. Initially the object of our attention is external; with practice we learn to internalize it, allowing it to rest in the center of our attention. Wholeheartedly embracing the object of our attention, we learn to rest with ease and tranquility in each moment.

GUIDED MEDITATION: CALMING THE MIND

For this meditation choose something that will serve as your meditation object. It can be a flower, a candle, a stone or leaf, or an object that symbolizes serenity and calmness for you. In the beginning it is best not to select anything that is overly complex or emotionally charged for you.

Place the object on the ground in front of your meditation place.

Let your body settle into a posture of calm alertness.

Gently close your eyes.

Take a few moments to soften your body, noticing the points where it connects with the ground, cushion, or chair.

Take a few slightly fuller breaths to establish your attention in the moment.

Now open your eyes and let your gaze rest gently on the meditation object in front of you.

Take a few moments to familiarize yourself with the object, noticing its textures, color, and shape.

Let your eyes rest gently on the object, not wandering the room to notice anything else. Whatever other sensations or thoughts appear, give them minimal attention, bringing a dedicated attention to connect with your meditation object.

Explore your object fully with your eyes and attention. Cultivate a patient intimacy with it. Notice its textures, color, and shape. Explore all the subtleties of it.

Now close your eyes and see if you can bring an image of that object to life in your attention. See if you are able to hold a visual impression of your object in your mind, sensing the same detail of shape, color, and texture.

Initially you may be only able to do this for a few moments. If the image begins to blur or fade in your mind, don't struggle to maintain it, simply open your eyes to visually connect with the object once more.

You may need to shift your attention from the inner impression to the visual object a number of times before you find yourself able to sustain the impression in your attention for longer periods of time.

As your attention deepens, you will find a greater ease in accessing the visual imprint of the object in your attention. The image will become increasingly clear in its detail and vividness.

Let your attention rest within it, fully connected with it.

Sense the calmness that begins to emerge with the deepening attention.

> Let your attention be absorbed into the image so that it fills the whole of your consciousness.
>
> If your attention becomes distracted, know that you can simply open your eyes and renew your connection visually with the object in front of you. Then close your eyes once more, recalling that image and resting within it.
>
> When you are ready, open your eyes and move out of your meditation posture.

Contemplation

It is said that wholehearted, unmixed attention is prayer. Contemplation is a means of highlighting the spiritual and life themes that are important to us.

Contemplation is a way of gathering our attention and consciously investigating sorrow, the causes of sorrow, and the path to the end of sorrow on a moment-to-moment level. Through contemplation we open our hearts and minds to the possibility of joy, peace, and profound understanding in this moment. Contemplation reminds us to live in a sacred way and to place at the center of our lives the aspiration to liberate our hearts and minds.

Aspiration is an essential part of every spiritual path. We do not practice meditation to stay the same or simply to become more intimately aware of the chaos and turbulence that burden our hearts and minds, we undertake a meditative path to seek for the stillness of mind and vastness of heart spoken of by all the great teachers and mystics of the past and present. We seek to explore the timeless teachings of peace, wisdom, and compassion within the context of our own lives.

In the busyness of our lives it is all too easy to neglect to listen to ourselves and to forget what it is that brings meaning and authenticity to every single thing that we undertake. We need to remember what makes our hearts sing, what gladdens our minds, and what inner values we treasure. All that we accomplish, achieve, and perform is truly meaningful only when it communicates the values we cherish in our hearts.

Each day, remembering what brings a deepening authenticity to our lives, we need to ask ourselves: Did I love well? Am I awake in my life? Did I remember to care for all the moments I lived? Was I present in my life today?

GUIDED MEDITATION: CONTEMPLATION

Each day take just a few moments to sit comfortably and be still within a posture of calm balance.

Let your mind and body relax, softening any areas of tension in your body and consciously letting go of the swirls of thought in your mind.

Gently close your eyes and rest in the stillness of your body.

Take a few moments to reflect on your day, sensing the times when you may have struggled or felt uneasy.

Just hold those events and moments in a kind and calm attention, not trying to resolve, justify, or explain them. Remember them without judgment or blame.

Reflect too on the moments in your day when you were truly

present and attentive—moments when you listened wholeheartedly to another person, reached out with generosity to care for another.

Place in the center of your attention a word, a phrase or a line from a sacred text and let it rest clearly and gently at the forefront of your attention.

It could be a simple word like "peace," "love," or "compassion."

It could be a phrase such as "letting go," "living wholeheartedly," "the nature of all things is to change," or "peace is our capacity to be with life just as it is."

Choose a word, phrase, or sentence that reminds you of your deepest intentions and values or that is evocative of what you truly treasure.

Try not to ponder on it, analyze it, or think about it. Simply gather your attention around the word or phrase and sense the responses that come from your mind and heart.

Your attention may wander many times. Just gently and calmly bring it back to the word or phrase you have chosen.

Other thoughts may arise that seem more urgent or important. Try not to be diverted by them. Gently let them go and come back to your chosen focus.

Plant the word or phrase in your consciousness just as you would plant a seed in the ground, then nurture it with your attention and presence.

With stillness, create a climate in which a deeper intuition can begin to emerge.

Let contemplation strengthen your sense of dedication to all that brings depth and meaning to your life.

When you are ready, open your eyes and come out of the posture.

CHAPTER 2

Taking our Seat

There is a great art in learning to integrate our mind, body, and the present moment. Different factors in our lives have the effect of creating a schism between our body, heart, and mind. Experiences of trauma, illness, pain, and busyness leave a lingering impact upon our bodies and when unattended to are often stored there, debilitating our ability to meet our life with openness and fearlessness.

When faced with illness or pain, our conditioned reaction is to attempt to divorce ourselves from our body, seeking ways to rid ourselves of discomfort. Yet denial of and resistance to pain make us increasingly prone to a life of fantasy, distractedness, and dreams of a better future.

Also, when our lives speed up and we become enmeshed in busyness, our bodies are often left to follow in the agitated wake of the plans, goals, and demands that preoccupy our minds. We experience the effects in stress, illness, and exhaustion.

Life teaches us about the interrelated nature of our bodies, emotions, and minds. We feel the impact of our thoughts and emotions in our bodies. When our minds are lost in obsession or we find ourselves caught in an emotional storm of anger, fear, or anxiety, we sense the way our bodies register that distress. We see the impact of changes in our bodies in the quality of mind we experience and in our emotional life. Both unexpected and chronic pain directly affect the state of our minds. The simple reality of aging, with all its implications, has a powerful impact upon our hearts and minds. We ignore this interrelatedness at our peril—the consequences are stress, illness, and fragmentation.

The Body

Many of us are not particularly sensitive to the life of our bodies until they demand our attention through messages of pain or illness. We often find ourselves living at a slight distance from where our bodies are—in thoughts of the future, in the destinations we are intent on reaching, in memories of the past, or simply lost in thought. Countless styles of meditation teach us to attend to the life of our bodies with greater care. We learn to listen to the messages that our bodies are relaying on a moment-to-moment level. With attention, we learn to bring our minds into our bodies, restoring wholeness and integration. Through being increasingly present within our bodies, we find that our capacity to sensitively attend to the life of our minds and emotions is greatly enhanced.

There are simple but profound lessons to be learned in attending to our bodies. The sensitivity, compassion, and wakefulness we nurture in relationship to our bodies will begin to pervade all of our relationships.

Skillful and wise attention is a direct path to a greater connectedness not only with our bodies but also with our entire experience of life in the moment. Calm, ease, and sensitivity rely upon this connection.

Learning to listen to our bodies with calm awareness, we heed their signals, learn to trust them and know with greater immediacy the moments when we move from ease and calm to agitation and dis-ease. In attending to our bodies with greater mindfulness, we deepen our capacity to listen to the whole of our lives in a non-judgmental and compassionate way. For many people, learning to be at home within their bodies, alert and mindful, is an art that challenges lifelong patterns of unconscious reaction and abandonment.

As we listen to the life of our bodies, we learn much. We learn about change, about acceptance and letting go, about mortality and the impossibility of trying to control life. We learn the gifts of attention, simplicity, compassion, and sensitivity. The skills we learn through attending to the life of our bodies are skills relevant to every dimension of our lives. We discover we can embrace the world of our emotions and thoughts, our relationships and all of the events we meet daily with the same attention, mindfulness, and sensitivity.

GUIDED MEDITATION:
THE BODY

Allow your body to settle into a posture of ease and relaxation.

Let your eyes close gently.

Bring your attention into your body.

Be aware of your abdomen as it rises and falls with each in- and out-breath. Steady your attention within that rhythm of breathing for a few minutes. Whenever your attention is pulled away into thoughts or images, just gently return it to your awareness of breathing.

Consciously let your whole body relax, softening any areas of tension or holding.

Now take your attention and focus it just on the top of your head, remaining alert to any sensations that are present in that part of your body. Don't expect anything special to be happening, just attune your attention to the life of your body.

Slowly expand your focus of attention, gently moving it over your head and face, sensing the different sensations that are present and the places where there is no visible sensation.

Slowly move your attention down through your body. Be aware of your neck and throat and shoulders.

Systematically begin a slow movement of attention down through both of your arms and into your hands.

Let the life of your body speak to you. Sense the range of sensations in that life—pleasant, unpleasant, and neutral—and be equally present within all the sensations that appear.

Notice when you begin to resist an unpleasant sensation in your body and explore the possibility of just returning a gentle attentiveness to that area of pain.

Sense the inclination to skip over the more neutral sensations and be willing just to accept them as they are.

If pleasant sensations appear in your body, notice the tendency to want to linger in those areas. Just notice the pleasant sensations and continue moving your attention through your body.

Return your attention to your neck and begin a conscious exploration of the trunk of your body, noticing how sensations appear and fade away. Some of those sensations may be strong and obvious, others subtle and quiet. Let go of the temptation to focus only on sensations that are intense while ignoring the subtler sensations.

Keep your attention moving, mindfully and slowly attending to every part of your body.

Let the downward movement of attention continue through your legs and into your feet.

In the moments when your attention is drawn away into thought, just gently return it to the area of your body you left and continue.

When your attention has arrived at the soles of your feet, consciously begin to move it back up through your body, following the same pathways you previously visited.

Be mindful of the quality of your attention as you move it through your body. Remain as calmly focused and sensitive as possible.

There may be many moments when you are aware of hurrying, judgment, or concepts arising in your mind. Gently let them go and return your attention to the direct experience of your body.

Release any expectations of having particular kinds of sensations. This is not a practice dedicated to altering or fixing anything within our bodies, but a practice of learning to find balance and equanimity with the life of our body, just as it is, moment to moment.

Continue to move your attention through your body for the duration of the meditation, heeding its signals and messages directly, and bringing calmness and sensitivity to whatever appears in your body.

When you are ready, open your eyes, rest for a moment and then gently move out of the posture.

Mapping the Landscape of Pain

Aging, sickness, and moments of pain are intrinsic to the life of all of our bodies. Bodily pain comes in many guises—some of it is chronic, some temporary, some unavoidable. Our first response is to resist it. We have numerous strategies to try to ward pain off, to avoid it, or camouflage it with distraction. Aversion, terror, and agitation interweave themselves with the experiences in our bodies and we are easily lost in dread and despair. Our bodies may even be seen as enemies, sabotaging our well-being and happiness. When we are enmeshed in this knot of fear and resistance, there is little space for healing or compassionate attention to occur.

And yet we can learn to touch discomfort and pain with an attention that is loving, accepting, and spacious. We can learn to befriend our bodies, even in the moments when they are most distressed and uncomfortable. We can discover that it is possible to release aversion and fear. With caring and curious attention, we can see that there is a difference between the sensations occurring in our bodies and the thoughts and emotions that react to those sensations. Instead of running from pain, we can bring a curious and caring attention into the heart of pain. In doing so, we discover that our well-being and inner balance are no longer sabotaged. Surrendering our aversion and resistance, we find that pain is no longer intimidating or unbearable.

No one would suggest that learning to work skillfully with pain is an easy task, however, or that meditation is a way to fix pain or make it go away. Sometimes we are overwhelmed and we can learn to accept this too. In moments when the intensity of pain seems unbearable it is fine to take our attention away from it and connect with a simpler focus of attention such as breathing or listening for a time. When our hearts and minds have calmed and feel more spacious, it is the right moment to return our attention to the areas of pain in the body.

There are also times when it is often possible to dissolve the layers of tension and fear that gather around pain and to embrace it with greater spaciousness and ease. We may even find a deep inner balance and serenity in the midst of pain. These are moments of great possibility and strength.

Working with pain, learning to accept and embrace it, is a moment-to-moment practice in which we release helplessness, despair, and fear. This is in itself healing and teaches us the way to find peace and freedom within the changing events of our bodies.

When pain or distress arises in our bodies our conditioned reaction is to pin it down and solidify it with concepts. We say "my knee," "my back," "my illness," and the floodgates of apprehension are opened. We predict a dire future for ourselves, fear the intensification of the pain, and at times dissolve into helplessness and despair. Our concepts serve both to make the pain more rigid and to undermine our capacity to respond to it skillfully. We are caught in the tension of wanting to divorce ourselves from a distressed body while the intensity of pain keeps drawing us back into our body.

Meditation offers a very different way of responding to pain in our bodies. Instead of employing strategies to avoid it or becoming lost in resistance and distress, we learn to investigate what is actually being experienced within our bodies calmly and curiously. Instead of aversion we can bring a compassionate, accepting attention directly to the core of pain. This is the first step towards healing and releasing the layers of agitation and dread that too often surround and serve to intensify pain.

Accepting the impossibility of divorcing ourselves from our body and the futility of trying to avoid pain, we can begin to investigate the landscape of pain. Turning our attention directly towards the distress or pain, we discover that the pain we had previously perceived as a solid mass of discomfort is in truth very different. Sensations are changing from moment to moment. There are different textures within those sensations—tightness, heat, pressure, burning, stinging, aching… As we ask, "What is this?" the label "pain" becomes increasingly meaningless.

Within all pain and distress we discover there are two levels of experience. One is the simple actuality of the sensation, feeling, or pain, and the other is our story of fear that surrounds it. Letting go of the story, we are increasingly able to connect with the simple truth of the pain with interest and balance. So we discover that it may be possible for us to find calmness and peace even in the midst of distress.

GUIDED MEDITATION:
MAPPING THE LANDSCAPE OF PAIN

Let your body settle into a posture that is relaxed and at ease. If you are sitting, try to keep your back and neck upright. If your body is very distressed, lie down comfortably on your back with a commitment to being fully awake and present.

Let your eyes close gently.

For a few moments just be aware of your entire body. Consciously soften any areas of tightness or tension. Move a gentle, curious attention slowly over your face, jaw, shoulders, and hands, allowing them to soften and relax.

Be aware calmly and intentionally of all the places your body contacts the floor, cushion, or chair, sensing the warmth or subtle pressure within those places of contact.

Expand your attention, becoming aware of your entire body resting in as much ease as possible. Bring a wholehearted attention to your body. Be aware of all the different sensations that are present. Sense the touch of the air on your skin and the touch of your clothes on your body. Let your awareness include your heart beating and the rising and falling of your chest and abdomen with your breathing. Sense too the multitude of different sensation happening within your body—tingling, warmth, movement, pleasant and unpleasant sensations…

Within the range of the different experiences, notice which sensations are most predominant, which area of your body stands out through the intensity of the sensation. This is the area asking for your attention.

Focus as fully as possible on that area of your body, tracing the edges of the discomfort with your attention, as if you were tracing the edges of a feature on a map.

Connect very directly with the sensations. Try to stay closely connected with the actual experience of the sensations in your body.

Notice where the edges of the pain or discomfort fade on the edges of the map and where different sensations are present, sensations of warmth, pressure, or movement.

Let your attention rest in those areas for some moments, noticing the sensations that are pleasant or neutral.

Notice the sensations present in your hands, the soles of your feet, all the parts of your body that are not in the map of pain.

Bring your attention back into the map and focus your attention very directly on where the sensations are most acute. Notice that there may be points of intensity surrounded by areas of tension or discomfort.

Move your attention into the center of the pain and notice its texture, whether tight, piercing, aching, or stabbing. Ask, "What is this?"

If you notice that your attention begins to become tight, aversive, or fearful, again move it to a part of your body that is outside the map of pain. Rest and focus your attention there once more, renewing your calmness and balance. Then return again to the points of pain within the map.

There may be a number of these points. Carefully move your attention from one to another, gently exploring each one. Notice what changes may be happening within those points of discomfort, how the sensations may be changing in texture or arising and passing.

Be patient with the exploration, not demanding that the pain disappears, but being simply willing to explore the truth of that sensation.

Whenever your attention becomes tight or aversive as you focus on areas of acute sensation, it is a clue to go outside the map of pain once more to focus on an area of your body that is relaxed and at ease. You are learning to visit pain, explore it, see it as it is, but always giving yourself permission to leave it.

End your meditation by returning once more to an awareness of your whole body, alert to the spectrum of sensation that comprises the life of your body.

Rest in that spacious awareness for some moments before opening your eyes and slowing coming out of your meditative posture.

Breathing into Pain

GUIDED MEDITATION:
BREATHING INTO PAIN

Let your body settle into a comfortable and relaxed posture. Once more just notice if there are any obvious areas of tightness or tension in your body and consciously soften and relax them. Sense your whole body relaxing and settling into the moment.

Let your eyes gently close.

Focus your attention in your abdomen and notice how it rises and falls with each in- and out-breath. Let your attention gently rest in that natural rhythm of expanding and relaxing. Don't force or alter your breathing in any way.

Keep your attention focused on the breathing in your belly, staying with each in-breath and each out-breath for its full duration.

With each out-breath sense the relaxing and softening of your body. Breathe out any tension.

When your attention wanders away from your abdomen, just gently return it without judgment or impatience.

Resting your attention within your breathing, listen to the signals your body is sending you. The strongest signals will be coming from the part of your body in the most pain.

As you breathe in, sense how that in-breath may go directly into the area of pain, as if you were breathing into your neck, back, or wherever your body is most acutely uncomfortable.

Sense your in-breath as a breath of cool air bathing the area of pain.

As you breathe out, sense yourself breathing out the heat of the pain.

Continue to focus on your breathing as if you are breathing in and through the heart of the pain itself.

Breathe in coolness and breathe out heat. Breathe in calm and breathe out tension.

Sense how the solidity of the pain may begin to soften and change.

There may be moments when the discomfort initially becomes more acute as you bring attention to it. Find the patience to stay there a little longer, continuing to breathe in and out of the discomfort. Allow your body to stay very relaxed and at ease. See if the intensity of the pain begins to dissolve.

If the pain continues to grow in intensity, simply return your attention to your abdomen for a time, once more aware of how it expands and relaxes with each breath. Let the steadiness of your attention on your abdomen be the path to restoring calmness and ease.

Allow yourself to shift your attention from the movement in your abdomen to breathing more consciously into the pain and back again. Do this as many times as you need to.

When you are ready, let your eyes open and slowly move out of the posture.

The Symphony of Pain

During times of severe illness or episodes of acute pain our bodies can be sending so many different signals of pain that it is impossible to isolate any one area of distress in our body. Like listening to a discordant symphony with all the instruments playing a different movement, we can feel ourselves bombarded by such an onslaught of pain that calmness and attention feel inaccessible. These are the times when we are most prone to becoming exhausted and dispirited. The distress in our body feels constant and solid. These are also the times when our minds are most prone to become contracted and tight. Our emotions of aversion and fear can appear as intensely as the pain in our bodies and we find ourselves fighting and struggling with the pain or illness, only wanting it to end. In these moments of intensity we can feel betrayed by our bodies, regarding them as saboteurs of our well-being.

The first step towards healing in these times of intensity is to loosen the bands of tightness that constrict our hearts and minds. Running from the pain is not a real possibility in these times of severe distress—it only exhausts us further. We come to understand that as difficult as it may appear, there is a great compassion in surrendering the fight and struggle.

What often helps in these moments is to cultivate a spacious, sensitive, and open awareness that embraces not only the surges of distress in our bodies, but also includes the world of sounds, sights, emotions, thought, and touch that are existing concurrently with the sensations of pain. Our world is not only pain, it is the constriction of our mind that blanks out a wider awareness of the moment. Cultivating a more spacious awareness creates a container in which the bodily distress can take its rightful place amongst the multitude of sensory impressions that are also part of our life. This spacious awareness can serve to soften the intensity of the identification and fear that have latched onto the pain.

GUIDED MEDITATION:
THE SYMPHONY OF PAIN

Find a position for your body, either sitting or lying, in which you find the greatest ease and relaxation.

Let your eyes close.

Intentionally relax all the parts of your body as far as you are able.

Sense the contact of your body with the ground or seat. Be aware of the warmth and pressure present in those points of contact.

Let your mind be as open and spacious as the sky and allow yourself simply to rest in that vastness.

With sensitivity, just be aware of everything that arises in that calm openness, just as you would be aware of clouds appearing in the sky.

Notice the thoughts, sounds, emotions, images and all the other sensations that enter into that open space, without judging or rejecting anything.

Notice how some of these may appear only momentarily, while others linger for a time.

From that place of openness, begin to consciously move your attention through the different sensory doors, visiting each one in turn, consciously attending to what is appearing at just that one moment.

Begin by taking your attention just to listening for a few moments, not looking for sound but resting in the simple experience of listening.

Notice the sounds that are near and far, the different textures of sound, the way that sounds appear, last for a time, then disappear. Just listen…

Now expand the field of your attention to be aware of your entire body. Notice how sensations, like sounds, appear, last for a time, then change into something else. Try to keep your attention very spacious, embracing your whole body, sensitive to the spectrum of sensations that are arising and passing. Some are intense and obvious, some subtle, some pleasant and some unpleasant.

Move your attention from one area of predominant sensation to the next, being wholeheartedly present with one sensation at a time.

Try not to judge or label any of them. Simply remain connected to the life of your body.

Now consciously turn your attention to what is happening in your mind. Notice how thoughts and images, like sounds and sensations, also appear and disappear in the openness of your awareness. Some of the thoughts are quiet, ephemeral, arising and passing so quickly they are hardly noticed. Other thoughts are harsh, demanding, and wish to linger for a time. With calmness and sensitivity, treat all of the thoughts and images equally, simply touching them with gentle attention.

Again come back to rest in an open, spacious awareness, embracing and attending to the fullness of your experience, one moment at a time.

If you find that your mind becomes constricted or tight, preoccupied with what is happening in your body, once more initiate a calm and gentle movement of attention through listening, turning your attention to body and mind, and cultivating space and openness.

When you are ready, open your eyes and gently move out of the posture.

The Emotion of Pain

Pain in our body, particularly chronic and acute pain, has an inevitable emotional impact that can be equally debilitating. Blame, fear, self-condemnation, despair, anxiety, and terror can arise in the wake of physical illness and root themselves in our bodies, further hindering our capacity to heal and find ease. We can become enraged with our bodies or even regard the presence of pain as a personal failing. The emotional and psychological reactions we bring to times of illness and distress further our inclination to distance ourselves from the moment that feels too painful and terrifying for us to be present in.

Our emotional reactions of fear and resistance often lodge themselves in our bodies alongside the pain, to the point where they are almost indistinguishable. Learning to notice the distinction between pain and our reaction to it, we will begin to see that although the pain in our bodies may not be optional, some of the pain of our reactions is optional.

The natural desire to avoid pain is translated in our minds and hearts into turbulence and anxiety, and our sense of inner balance is swept away in the avalanche of those feelings. Even when we are fortunate in that our body recovers, without mindfulness the emotions associated with illness or pain linger much longer in our bodies and minds. We may begin to live in a fearful way, treating every unpleasant sensation as a messenger of doom, assuming it signals a return of the pain or illness. The damage we do to ourselves in ignoring the impact of our emotional reactions compounds our tendency to feel anxious and afraid.

There is a great art in learning to be present with pain or illness, just as it is, in the moment when it arises. But with mindfulness, we can learn to make peace with pain. We can learn to be present in just one moment at a time and so liberate ourselves from the dread of what the next moment may bring. We can learn the kindness of acceptance rather than the harshness of denial.

GUIDED MEDITATION:
THE EMOTION OF PAIN

Let your body settle into a position of ease and relaxation.

Gently close your eyes.

Spend a few minutes tracing the movement of your breath in your body, from its beginning to its end.

Pay particular attention to following your out-breath to its very end. With each out-breath let your body soften and relax. With each out-breath feel the release of tightness and tension.

Now expand your attention to be aware of your whole body and all the different sensations that are arising and passing in it.

Spend some minutes just calmly attending to the spectrum of sensations you feel—the pleasant, the unpleasant, and the neutral.

Now bring your attention to an area of your body that has been injured, painful, or ill in the past or in the present—it might be your heart, your back or neck, or any part of your body that has occupied your attention in a painful way.

As you focus on that part of your body, sense what emotions or images might arise.

Be aware of any feelings of fear, anger, tightness, or resistance that appear.

Notice if they affect your body. Your breathing might begin to tighten, your shoulders or jaw might begin to tense. You might notice a hardening in your stomach or tension in your neck or face.

Take your attention gently, without judgment, directly to the part of your body that is registering the emotion, and if possible make a quiet mental note of what it is.

Note simply, "This is anger," or "This is fear."

Explore the sensation of the emotion in your body, seeing how it changes. Place your attention directly within the feeling, without judgment or trying to get rid of it in any way.

Sense the anger, fear, apprehension, or judgment registering in the sensations in your body.

Sense whether it is possible for you to accept the emotion just as it is, to make peace with it.

It too is changing, inviting a compassionate attention.

If memories, thoughts, or judgments begin to flood your mind, just go back to being aware of your breathing for a few minutes.

When you feel there is once more a greater sense of calmness, return your attention to your body and its companion emotions.

Ask yourself whether it is possible for you to welcome, accept, and make peace with those emotions.

When you are ready, open your eyes and gently come out of the posture.

Releasing Stress

When we use the word "stress" everyone immediately knows what it is we are talking about. Yet stress is a generic term that attempts to describe a multi-dimensional and complex experience. It is not just a static state of mind, but a process that describes the way we are interacting and interfacing with the world around us and within us. We can feel stressed by work pressures, by goals, the needs or expectations of others, and by time. We can feel stressed by the weight of our own thoughts, unfulfilled wants, conflicting emotions, and the quality of our bodies. Stress is what happens when an overburdened mind adversely impacts upon our bodies and incapacitates us in our ability to meet life calmly and wholeheartedly.

Stress is symptomatic of an underlying disharmony in ourselves and our lives. It is a messenger asking us to examine what we are neglecting or not giving attention to. Much of the stress we experience may be much more optional than we initially believe. We can all learn to attend to our life with greater wholeheartedness, to let go with more ease and to care for the moment we are in.

A meditation teacher was once asked about the right amount of time to give to meditation. His answer was that half an hour was fine except in times of exceptional busyness, then an hour was needed.

Too often we misinterpret stress as a signal to do and accomplish more. Yet we need to listen to stress as an indicator of our need to slow down, attend to each moment with greater care, and release the haste that has come to govern our minds and lives. We cannot afford to ignore the signals that it is sending us—tension, agitation and anxiety.

Meditation is not a quick-fix solution for stress. Ease, clarity, effectiveness, and sensitivity in our lives will not arise from a mind and heart that are overburdened. Thoughts, choices, words, and actions born of an agitated mind will invariably be themselves agitated and anxious, and rarely bring the consequences or results we are seeking.

Our conditioned response to stress is to go faster or to hide. We try to do more, accomplish more, or simply flee. None of these responses are effective in teaching us to live a more easeful, creative, and sensitive life. In the midst of feeling stressed it rarely occurs to us that what is needed is for us to stop and be still, yet this is this most instrumental and effective way to heal our bodies, minds, and lives. The moments of greatest tension, anxiety, and agitation are the very moments to which we are asked to bring a mindful attention. Finding the willingness to stop and be still provides the opportunity to meet the internal and external dynamics that are creating havoc in our lives. We see that it is not just the factors of time, demands, people, or even our own thoughts that intrinsically possess the power to stress us. Stress and ease both lie within how we perceive and respond to everything that life brings to us.

Stress is what happens when the multiplicity of events in our life and our reactions to them mass together into a form of inner gridlock. Eventually we find ourselves stuck in an inner paralysis—unable to respond well to even the smallest details. Life feels impossible—everything appears to be too much to respond to. We feel we are facing an impenetrable mass of need, demand, and pressure.

This is in truth a state of mind and not a description of reality. We need to learn to unpack the solidity of that perception. We can pay attention to one moment, one event and one impression at a time. We can learn to calm our bodies and explore with attention what it is we might be able to let go of in our minds. We can learn to pay attention to the beginnings and endings that are part of all our internal and external events. Stress is born of not feeling able to let go of events that have already passed or our thoughts and apprehensions of events that are yet to arise. We can learn to meet the moment we are in wholeheartedly and to let it go as it passes.

GUIDED MEDITATION:
RELEASING STRESS

Find a position for your body in which you feel deeply relaxed and at ease.

Let your eyes gently close and for a few moments just focus on your breathing, noticing the beginning of each breath and the end of each breath.

Follow each out-breath to its very end, sensing it dissolving into space.

Let yourself rest in that momentary pause between the end of one breath and the beginning of another.

Expand your attention and listen to what is happening in your body and mind in that moment.

Notice how many of your thoughts are preoccupied with events, people, meetings, and experiences that are not actually present in that moment. Sense this without judgment or resistance and see whether it is possible for you to gently release those thoughts and return to an awareness of breathing.

Notice the waves of agitation, tension, or anxiety that arise with the thoughts of the past and future and how they may be impacting on your body.

Come back once more to an awareness of your breathing.

Resting in calmness and ease, consciously invite into your mind an event, person, or experience that you have been preoccupied with or obsessing about.

Surround that thought with a mindful attention. Look at it directly. Can you see it as just a thought, an event in the mind?

Sense how that event in your mind is co-existing in this moment with countless other events—sounds, sensations in your body—and how they are all arising and passing together.

Move your attention between the thought, the sounds, and the bodily sensations that are present in this moment.

Notice how they all appear, last for a time, and then begin to fade or turn into something else.

Sense the natural rhythm of this arising and passing.

Notice how when any of these events are surrounded by aversion, agitation, or resistance, their lifespan is extended. When the surrounding reactions are released, the events find their place again in the natural rhythm of arising and passing.

Attend mindfully not only to the events that appear in your mind and body, but also to those subtle pauses and places of stillness between events.

Just as you are able to notice the momentary pause between an out-breath and the next in-breath, sense what is present after the fading away of a sound, a thought, or a bodily sensation.

Allow yourself to rest in the pauses and sense the possibility of resting in all the events that arise in your mind and body.

When you are ready, let your eyes open and move out of the posture.

Sustaining Attention: Contact Points

There is a great art not only in being able to connect with the life of your body, but also in being able to sustain your attention within your body. Initially as you are present within your body you may find your attention is persistently jumping away and moving into the world of thoughts, the past and the future. The movement from applied attention to sustained attention is one of the greatest challenges in meditation.

Through constantly applying our attention to our bodies and gently returning our attention to our bodies in all the moments when it becomes lost in thought, our capacity to be present and at ease within our bodies deepens.

This process can become effortless and joyful. Sustained attention refreshes and renews us, and is an art that we are increasingly able to bring to all of the events and activities of our lives. In sustained attention our hearts and minds discover true depths of spaciousness, serenity, and clarity.

GUIDED MEDITATION: CONTACT POINTS

Settle into a posture that is as relaxed and alert as possible. Let your back and neck be upright and your hands rest gently together.

Let your eyes gently close.

Take a few moments just to be aware of your whole body, sensing deeply its stillness and uprightness.

Be aware too of all of the different sensations that appear and pass through your body moment to moment.

Select just a few contact points that you are aware of in your body—the touch of your backside on the pillow or chair, the touch of your hands together, the touch of your knees on the ground or the contact of your feet with the ground.

Move your attention to the touch of your hands together. Sustain your attention there for some moments, noticing all of the different sensations that are present and the ways in which they change.

After a few minutes move your attention to the next contact point, the touch of your backside on the chair or cushion. Again sustain your attention in that point.

Every time your attention moves away to a thought or a sensation in a different part of your body, gently return it to the contact point you are currently focused on.

Sense all of the sensations in that contact point from within your body, feeling them wholeheartedly.

After some minutes, bring your attention to the next contact point, the touch of your knees or feet on the ground. Be very steady with your focus, noticing both the obvious and the subtle sensations present in that point of contact.

After some minutes, return your attention to the touch of your hands together.

Continue the movement of your attention back from one contact point to the next, without hurrying or anticipating what comes next.

Let your attention rest deeply within your body. Each time you are drawn to a thought or image, make a quiet but firm resolve to come back to the contact point, sustaining your connection with it.

When you are ready, open your eyes and come out of the posture.

Inner Peace

Peace is not the absence of challenge or difficulty, but the release of judgment and fear. It begins in our own hearts, minds, and lives. We cannot control or govern the hearts and minds of another, but we can reclaim our own capacity to be at peace with all things, including ourselves. Learning to make peace with ourselves is the first step in understanding what it means to be at peace with all things.

It is not difficult for us to see that our relationships with other people frequently mirror the kind of relationship we have with our own bodies, minds, and hearts. If we are prone to be judgmental or dismissive of others, it may be worthwhile to explore the ways in which we are judgmental or dismissive of ourselves. The impatience, frustration, expectancy, or blame that may sabotage our relationship with all those who are part of our lives will likely have their roots in the ways in which we relate to our own inner world.

If we wish to nurture relationships of kindness, understanding, and intimacy in our lives it may be important to acknowledge that our relationship with ourselves is the classroom in which we learn the arts of generosity, tolerance, care, and tenderness. Wherever we go in this life, whether alone or with others, we can never divorce ourselves from our own hearts and minds. The longings we treasure for intimacy, oneness, and friendship with others rest upon our capacity to cross the abyss of distance and fear that can separate us from ourselves.

Peace in our lives is not separate from our capacity to make peace with ourselves. Serenity in our lives rests upon our capacity to make peace with the inner struggles that devastate the calmness of our own hearts and minds. Peacemaking begins with our capacity to release ourselves from the conflicts and struggles we carry in our relationship to ourselves.

GUIDED MEDITATION:
INNER PEACE

Settle into a posture that is as relaxed and alert as possible.

Allow your eyes to gently close.

Take a few moments to be aware of your body, releasing any areas of tension. Let your shoulders, face, and hands relax and soften.

For a few moments focus your attention on your breathing. Be particularly aware of your outgoing breath, following it with your attention until the very end of the breath.

Rest your attention in the brief moment between the ending of an out-breath and the beginning of the next in-breath.

Take a few moments to reflect on where you most repetitively battle with yourself.

Sense the places you are most judgmental of yourself, the places where you extend to yourself the greatest unkindness or blame, the places that trigger feelings of shame or self-consciousness.

You may be aware of carrying events or acts from the past in your heart and mind that are laden with guilt or regret.

You may be aware of recurring patterns in your present, in speech, thought, or action, that cause pain or alienation and that you wish to be free from.

As you reflect on these patterns or events, sense what happens in your body and mind.

Sense how simply bringing these places of pain into your attention may trigger feelings of contraction, tension, or resistance in your body. You may be aware of the rhythm of your breathing changing, becoming shorter or tighter. If this happens, bring your attention to the part of your body that is registering distress or discomfort and let it soften and relax.

Sense the aversion you have for these places in your own heart and mind. Sense your wish to be free from them. Be aware of how the aversion and resistance themselves are the energy of struggle and inner estrangement.

Reflect on what you may need to cultivate or nurture to make peace with yourself.

Reflect on what difference it would make to those places of rejection and alienation to cultivate a greater kindness, acceptance, or compassion.

Can you offer to yourself the forgiveness and generosity of heart to embrace the places of greatest difficulty and unease in your own heart and mind?

Are you able to stay present with those places in yourself that you are most tempted to flee from?

Reflect on what it might mean to befriend yourself, to offer to yourself the openness and understanding you would both wish to offer to others and to receive from others.

Sense that your capacity to make peace with yourself may not depend upon denying anything.

Your capacity to be at peace with yourself begins with your willingness to let go of prejudice and judgment.

With a wholehearted and gentle attentiveness, explore those places in your heart and mind that are the source of the greatest struggle and pain.

Sense how it may be possible to bring calmness, gentleness, and care to those places without any expectation.

When you are ready, open your eyes and come out of the posture.

Peacemaking

The possibilities of conflict in our world are evident and endless. The opportunities for making peace are also countless. It is too vast and idealistic a notion to take on the task of solving every area of conflict and war in the world, but it is realistic and possible for each of us to examine our own lives and relationships and see the places we are asked to make peace with.

War, violence, oppression, and prejudice must all be challenged with courage and compassion. At the same time a genuinely awake and spiritual life asks us to honestly face the moments and places where our own hearts and minds are governed by anger, hatred, and violence.

Walking a path of peace, inwardly and outwardly, we first turn our attention to our own lives. On a theoretical and idealistic level it is easy for us to promote and advocate peace. But what of those we see as enemies, judge, dismiss, or exile from our hearts? It is in the face of all these that we learn the true lessons of peacemaking.

We can feel divided and apart from so many people in our life and world. We fear or avoid those who have harmed us in the past or appear to hold the power to harm us in the present. We are prone to judge and dismiss those whose opinions, beliefs, and creeds are different from our own. We may find ourselves condemning countless people in our world, people we do not even know, for their acts, words, or for all the actions they neglect to do.

Anger, judgment, and fear are heavy burdens for our hearts and minds to carry, and antagonism and rage will only perpetuate the cycles of division that scar our world. Peace begins in our willingness to find a different way of being with all the people in our world who enrage, offend, or hurt us. Peacemaking is a moment-to-moment exploration that we can invite in whenever we find ourselves traveling the familiar pathways of hatred, prejudice, fear, and anger.

Peacemaking asks for profound courage and commitment. We begin to make peace by turning our attention to our own communities, families, and relationships. It is the people from whom we feel estranged that we are asked to embrace with our attention, understand, and befriend. This is the beginning of healing—the healing not only of that schism, but the healing of our own heart.

GUIDED MEDITATION: PEACEMAKING

Settle your body into a posture of calmness and ease.

Let your eyes gently close.

Take a few moments to be aware of your body. If there are areas of tension or tightness, gently relax them.

Be aware of the stillness of your body. Sense the natural rhythm of your breath moving within your body.

With each out-breath, let your mind calm, releasing any preoccupations or busyness.

Reflect for a moment on all the ways you treasure peace. Connect with your own longing to be free from conflict and harm, your longing for safety, acceptance, and understanding.

Consciously invite into your attention a person in your life you are currently struggling with or feel alienated from.

As you hold an image of them in your attention, remembering them as clearly as you can, sense the feelings that may arise in response to that image—fear, anger, mistrust, resistance...

Hold those feelings gently, without judgment or blame, and sense their pain and heaviness.

Sense how they impact on your body and how they provoke all the old stories of anger or hurt in your mind.

Simply hold that world of tightness and pain in a warm and caring attention.

Ask yourself what would be needed to let go of that pain, resistance, or fear. Would you need to let go of your stories about that person, your desire for vengeance, or your fear of them?

Would it be possible for you to find in yourself a greater generosity, loving kindness, or forgiveness?

What would it mean to let go of the judgments and to seek to understand the life, heart, and mind of another?

If you find that your mind and heart begin to be overwhelmed by painful emotions, just come back to rest your attention in your breathing and your body for a time.

When you are ready, renew your connection with the person you find difficult and again explore the possibility of that relationship being radically different than it is at this time.

Sometimes it is useful to visualize that person as an infant or as an aged and frail person facing the same life uncertainties that you face, sharing with you the longing for kindness and care.

Again ask yourself what can be released in your own heart so that the difficult person is no longer seen as an enemy.

Let the questions rest softly in your attention, without demanding an answer. Listen to your own heart's response and the wisdom of your own mind.

When you are ready, open your eyes.

As you go into your day, take with you the commitment to make peace with all things, to be at peace with yourself and with all of the people who touch your life.

CHAPTER 3

Awakening the Heart

We all long to live with an awakened and loving heart. Our lives are enriched and given meaning by the love, compassion, generosity, and joy we find within our own hearts.

Life itself will ask us to find openness and vastness of heart. Each of us will be asked to respond to sometimes unbearable moments of hardship and heartbreak. We will all be deeply affected by events of pain, terror and alienation. Our hearts can be shattered by emotional storms of anger, fear, grief, and hatred. Yet it is also within our hearts that we find the strength and fearlessness that can both reach out to heal another and embrace the challenges in our own lives. The times of greatest confusion and turmoil live within our own hearts, but so too do the times of greatest joy and openness.

An awakened heart loves deeply, cares fully, and is committed to the qualities of compassion, generosity, and forgiveness—the qualities that heal sorrow. Meditative disciplines and traditions offer a number of classical practices that are dedicated to awakening our hearts and deepening our understanding of love and compassion. These practices can be undertaken both in formal meditation and in all the moments of engagement and relationship in our lives.

An awakened heart does not demand evidence that our love and compassion are producing particular effects or results. It acknowledges that it is the depth of our caring and our commitment to loving and healing that enrich us and serve to heal every moment and experience of conflict and estrangement in our world.

Forgiveness

Our hearts and minds can be tormented by storms of hatred, anger, resentment, and fear. They can equally be healed by the power of forgiveness. Our common bond as human beings is our capacity both to be hurt and to hurt others.

In our life we will face difficult situations in which we may be insulted, humiliated, dismissed, or rejected. These are all painful experiences that can fester in our hearts, poisoning our capacity to trust and care and leaching joy from our lives. We can carry these moments of pain through the whole of our lives.

Fearing and resenting those who have harmed us, in truth we often think more about them than the people we love. We can expend considerable energy planning strategies of retaliation or self-protection. We can find ourselves obsessing about experiences that have long passed, while those who have harmed us may be oblivious to the impact they have had upon us. We can live our lives in regret and bitterness, which is often to forget to live at all. A wounded heart and all the fears and apprehensions born of that hurt can seem to create an eternal prison. And though the pain may have been inflicted upon us by another, we are perhaps the only ones who can release ourselves from that prison of resentment and fear.

We may also encounter times in our lives when it feels deeply difficult to forgive not only others but also ourselves. We may have harmed another person through our words, actions, unconsciousness, or insensitivity, and we sense the divide of mistrust, fear, and anger that now separates us from that person. We cannot undo the acts that have been done, we cannot take back the words that have been spoken. So guilt, regret, and remorse become part of our lives. Storms of thought are born, beginning with the phrases "if only" and "I wish," and taking up space in our minds.

Forgiveness does not condone or justify the unjust, harmful, or unacceptable. But with wise forgiveness may come the resolve never to permit any past harm to be repeated in the present or future. It is not easy to forgive, but it is less painful than continuing to carry the burden of a painful past into all the remaining moments of our lives. So forgiveness is a way of releasing our own hearts from pain. It allows us to live a life in which we no longer carry the burdens of the past or endlessly replay the past in the present. We are released into a present that is no longer defined by the past. It is here that we find peace and the capacity to live with openness and trust.

Forgiveness is built upon patience, tolerance, and acceptance—qualities we extend to both ourselves and others. In doing so, we do not erase the imprints of pain from our own hearts or the hearts of others. Forgiveness is often a long journey that asks us to meet the hurt of betrayal, loss, and anger over and over. In each of these meetings we see the choices we face: we can linger in what has gone by and suffer, or we can meet that pain with understanding, compassion, and courage, and find a heart of ease. The forgiving heart is also a free heart.

Forgiveness for Ourselves

In our lives we can harm and abandon ourselves in countless ways—physically, emotionally, and psychologically. Through feelings of worthlessness, habit, and self-judgment we forget how to care for ourselves. For many people it is easier to care for others than to care for themselves. But through being overly busy, needing the approval and affirmation of others, and judging ourselves we can sabotage our well-being. The trail of regret and anxiety burdens our hearts, undermining our capacity to hold our own body, mind, and heart in an embrace of sensitivity and compassion in the present. We need to forgive ourselves for all the harm or hurt we may have inflicted on ourselves.

We must also learn to forgive ourselves for the harm we have done to others. Out of unconsciousness, fear, and anxiety we can speak, think and act in ways that hurt others, that make others fear us. The words we have spoken and the actions we have engaged in cannot be undone. Yet we can do what is possible to reconcile ourselves with the person we have hurt and forgive ourselves for our past insensitivity.

Forgiveness for ourselves rests upon our capacity to let go of what has already gone by and find a new beginning in the present. We can learn in our meditation to move from insensitivity and unconsciousness to a sensitivity and awareness that is both healing and freeing.

GUIDED MEDITATION:
FORGIVENESS FOR OURSELVES

Take some moments to find a posture of calmness and ease.

Let your eyes close and consciously soften all the parts of your body that feel tight or contracted.

Let your breathing relax and find its own natural rhythm.

Let your attention rest in the center of your chest, in the area of your heart, and just sense the life of your body in that area.

Cultivate an attentiveness of sensitivity and calm.

Take some moments to reflect on the ways that you may harm or hurt yourself through thought, word, or action.

Receive with kindness the images, memories, or bodily feelings that may arise, even if they are deeply painful.

Sense how those images, memories, or feelings belong to actions, words, and thoughts that have already passed.

In the present, let go of any form of self-judgment, guilt, or anxiety over what has in truth passed. Reflect on what forgiveness might mean in this moment, what it might mean to release the burden of the past and all that you regret.

Let your attention rest in the heart center, at the center of your chest, without demand or expectation.

Let these phrases rest softly in your attention and your heart:

"I forgive myself."

"I forgive myself for the words, actions, or thoughts that caused harm to myself, whether intentional or unintentional."

"I forgive myself for any way that I have hurt myself through fear, pain, or confusion."

"I forgive myself."

> Continue for some minutes to rest your attention in these phrases. Sense in your heart the possibility of letting go of the past, of learning new pathways of respect, kindness, and compassion for yourself.
>
> Memories and images laden with regret may arise. You can also allow them to pass and return to a forgiving heart.
>
> When you are ready, open your eyes and come out of the posture.

Asking Forgiveness from Others

Out of confusion, fear, and pain we can hurt others both through action and inaction. In fear and anger we can strike out at another as a way of trying to protect ourselves. Lost in confusion, we don't always appreciate the hurtful impact our words or actions have on the heart of another, except in retrospect. Then we can carry the legacy in our hearts throughout our lives. Regret and shame can dominate our inner story as we struggle with guilt and remorse.

At times our inaction can cause as much pain as our actions. We remember the times when we failed to reach out to another in need, we recall the words of comfort we never said and the times when we turned away from a person in pain out of fear or a sense of inadequacy. Just as we need to forgive ourselves for the confusion and fear that guided us in those moments of neglect, so we can also ask forgiveness from another. Asking for forgiveness from others can be a powerful way of recommitting ourselves to sensitivity, integrity, and care in the present.

Guided Meditation:
Asking Forgiveness from Others

Let your body relax into a posture of ease and balance.

Close your eyes if it enables you to focus more wholeheartedly.

Spend some moments focusing on your breathing.

With each out-breath, sense the release of any agitation or busyness within your mind.

Let the memories, images, and emotions arise in your heart of the times when you may have wounded, hurt, or neglected another. They may be memories of hurtful words you have spoken or hurtful ways of relating to another person through rage, fear, or jealousy.

Sense the heaviness of those images and feel your own sorrow and regret.

Numerous people and situations of pain may arise. Make room for them, one by one.

Sense the possibility of releasing this burden and healing these wounds.

Silently forgive yourself, letting these phrases of forgiveness rest in your heart:

"I forgive myself."

"I forgive myself for any hurt or suffering I may have caused you by my words, actions, or thoughts."

"I forgive myself for neglecting to care for you when it was asked of me."

"I forgive myself."

Let your attention rest in the phrases for a time and then turn your attention to those whom you would ask forgiveness of.

Invite into your heart and attention anyone from the past or present you feel you have hurt through action or inaction, whether intentional or unintentional.

Invite them to take a seat in your meditation and let your attention rest in these phrases:

"For any way I have caused you pain or hurt, I ask your forgiveness."

"For any way I have neglected you, I ask your forgiveness."

"For any way I have made you fear me, I ask your forgiveness."

Let your attention rest within those phrases for a time, with sincerity bridging the gap that exists between you and the other person, a gap born of pain or neglect.

As you rest your attention in the phrases, try not to become lost in the story of past pain and hurt. Come back to the present, come back to the sincerity and simplicity of the phrases.

Let go of the guilt or regret as you recommit yourself to kindness and integrity in the present.

When you are ready, open your eyes and come out of the posture.

This meditation on forgiveness is one you can return to as often as it feels helpful. Don't expect anything special to happen, simply bring a gentle attention into the dimensions of your heart and mind that are clouded by emotional pain and regret.

Forgiveness for Those Who Have Caused Pain

It is not easy for us to forgive those who have caused hurt or suffering to us or to others. It is not easy for us to sense the anger, fear, and confusion that drive those acts and words that can so deeply damage. It is truly challenging to open our hearts to those whom we fear, despise, and judge for the pain they have caused. Yet forgiveness asks us to cultivate understanding; it is an invitation to intimacy rather than alienation. Forgiveness is choosing a path of healing rather than abandonment and division.

In the absence of forgiveness, people who have harmed us can govern our hearts and lives. We think about them, dwell upon the ways they have hurt us, and allow them to shape our present through fear and anger. The incidents, words, and acts that have wounded us deeply may belong to a distant past, yet they can continue to dominate our present. We can find ourselves endlessly replaying them. Forgiveness releases us from this prison of fear and anger. Forgiving those who cause pain is in truth a way of protecting and healing ourselves.

Forgiving those who hurt us does not mean, however, that we should ever place ourselves in situations of danger or peril, nor does it mean justifying or condoning actions or words that are clearly harmful. We all need to find the courage and clarity to bring about the end of anything that violates and damages our world. We also need to find the mercy and compassion to embrace and understand those who cause pain. Then the wall of anger, hatred, and fear that can so powerfully divide us from one another can begin to melt in the light of forgiveness.

Forgiveness for those who have harmed us asks for a powerful generosity of heart. It is often helpful to begin with a case where the barriers of fear and anger do not feel so solid. We need to find deep inner resources of balance and courage to approach those who have most deeply wounded us. Sometimes we are simply not ready to reach out with forgiveness and understanding to a person who has hurt us deeply. But we can forgive ourselves for that reluctance and fear until a time comes when we feel more inwardly healed and renewed and we are able to forgive another.

Forgiving those who have harmed us is in fact a profound act of compassion for ourselves. It allows us to move on, unburdened by fear and anger, and embrace our present wholeheartedly. In forgiveness we are releasing ourselves from the tortured world of blame, anger, and hatred. As we forgive those who cause suffering, what we are in truth forgiving are the powerful forces of confusion, ignorance, fear, and anger that can blight any of our lives.

GUIDED MEDITATION:
FORGIVENESS FOR THOSE WHO HAVE CAUSED PAIN

Find a position for your body that is relaxed and free from tension.

Gently close your eyes.

Bring your attention into your body, consciously softening any places that feel tight or contracted.

Pay particular attention to your face and jaw, your neck, shoulders and hands, letting them relax fully.

Bring a gentle and calm attention to rest in your chest, in your heart area.

Invite into your attention someone who has hurt you, whether in small or deep ways.

Hold that person in your attention and sense the array of images and emotions that arise, without judging any of them. Let them rest in your heart and mind without grasping hold of any of them.

Sense the ways in which you have felt harmed or abandoned,

intentionally or unintentionally, by that person.

Feel the pain you carry with you from this past and sense that it may be time to lay down this burden.

Holding the difficult person in your attention, gently begin to offer the intention of forgiveness with the phrases:

"I forgive you for the pain you have caused."

"I forgive the anger, confusion, and ignorance at the heart of your harmfulness."

"To you who have hurt me, I offer forgiveness."

As you rest your attention in the phrases and intentions of forgiveness, sense whether even the tiniest glimmers of release or opening may be possible.

Sense the new beginnings that may be possible for you as you release the weight of the past.

You may find it difficult to stay connected with the image or memory of someone who has hurt you deeply. Do not be harsh with demands on yourself. If you begin to flounder in the memories of pain, just return your attention to your body and breathing. Let your body relax and soften, and when you are ready, come back to the phrases, again offering forgiveness.

When you are ready, open your eyes.

In cultivating forgiveness we need to respect the limits of our own hearts. It may be too soon for us to forgive. We may still be too wounded to open our hearts to someone who has hurt us. At these times we can learn just to visit the places where our hearts feel most raw or painful, to acknowledge the need to heal these tender places of division and pain, and to learn the kindness and power of forgiveness for ourselves and for all those who, through ignorance and confusion, cause pain.

Loving Kindness

Loving kindness embraces the qualities of acceptance, generosity, friendliness, and warmth we long to receive from others. It describes an unconditional warmth and care that we are able to extend to all those who are part of our lives—those we cherish and love, those we are indifferent to, those we feel most separate from, and our own selves. Cultivating loving kindness, we discover that the walls of mistrust and fear that can so painfully separate us from others can also begin to crumble. In developing our own capacities for fearlessness, tenderness, and benevolence, our lives are lived with greater ease and connectedness. The small gestures of love we receive from others nurture and heal us, while the gestures and words of love and kindness we are able to offer to others bring depth and intimacy to all of our relationships. Loving kindness awakens and gladdens our hearts.

We all know the power that ill will, anger, and fear have to damage and scar our lives and our world. Individuals, communities, and nations are divided by mistrust, fear, and rage. Our whole world cries out for greater generosity, tenderness, and love. Its divisions and conflicts will not be healed by yet more formulas, prescriptions, and strategies, but through a radical change in each of our hearts.

We share with all living beings the longing to be happy and free from pain and fear. We share with all living beings the yearning to be accepted, loved, and cared for. In the face of anger our tendency is to withdraw, close down, or disconnect from the person before us. Gripped by the rage or hurt present in our own hearts, we are prone to strike out, to harm another or exile them from our lives. The division, mistrust, and alienation that follow scar our lives and relationships. Our own anger and fear will lead us to commit countless acts that are born of unconsciousness and reactivity and lead to sorrow and alienation.

Loving kindness meditation teaches us how to find a refuge of calm openness within our own hearts. It is a refuge that protects us from fear, anger, and turmoil. With loving kindness meditation we learn to remember, honor, and cultivate the capacity each of us has to touch our world with warmth and friendliness. We nurture a sanctuary of balance and strength within ourselves that allows us to turn towards pain and adversity and heal division.

In loving kindness meditation we cultivate, again and again, the intention to embrace all moments with generosity and warmth. Yet loving kindness is not sentimentality, or even a particular kind of feeling. Simply in each moment we nurture our capacity for intimacy and understanding. Loving kindness meditation is a practice of happiness.

Loving Kindness for Oneself

Traditionally, loving kindness meditation begins with ourselves. We learn to offer an unconditional warmth, acceptance, and tenderness to our own bodies, minds, and hearts. Many people find it easier to extend love and care to others than to receive it or to offer that same generosity of heart to themselves. Historical feelings of worthlessness or inadequacy at times make us feel we are undeserving of love and tenderness. Loving kindness meditation can heal those historical wounds that impair our capacity to offer to ourselves the boundless generosity, acceptance, and tenderness that make our hearts sing.

In learning to extend loving kindness to ourselves we discover the freedom of heart born of letting go of the painful judgments, expectations, and demands. Cultivating loving kindness for ourselves is also the training ground for learning the lessons of the patience, attentiveness, tolerance and warmth that we would wish to pervade all of our relationships.

Classically, loving kindness is developed through establishing our attention in a few simple phrases that embody the intentions for the happiness and well-being we treasure. The phrases remind us of the possibility of making our inner home in a place of fearlessness, warmth, and balance instead of one of confusion or ill will. The practice is not a mechanical repetition of empty words, but a genuine offering of kindness and love in each moment.

Loving kindness meditation can be developed in a dedicated posture and time; it can also be cultivated in all the moments and circumstances of our lives that ask for healing and connectedness and invite us to nurture a loving heart.

GUIDED MEDITATION: LOVING KINDNESS FOR ONESELF

Find a position that is relaxed and comfortable. You can develop this practice in any posture, though you may find that sitting upright helps you to be more alert and attentive.

Let your eyes close and take some moments to consciously relax your body, softening any areas of holding or tension.

For a few minutes focus a gentle, alert attentiveness on your breathing, letting your mind and body calm with each out-breath.

Bring your attention to rest in the center of your chest, in the area of your heart.

Silently repeat the simple phrases of loving kindness, sensing the meaning of each one:

"May I be free from fear and danger."

"May I be happy."

"May I be peaceful."

Let each phrase rest gently in your heart and mind, taking care not to hurry the words, simply offering to yourself your heartfelt wishes for your well-being and happiness.

Don't expect that any particular feeling will arise. Simply allow the phrases and their meaning to fill your heart and mind.

If you wish, you can alter the words so that you are using phrases that have a personal meaning for you.

Expand your attention to be aware of your body, sensing all the pain and well-being your body can experience in this life. Youth, aging, health, illness, birth, and death are held within all of our bodies.

Holding your body in your awareness, continue to rest your attention in the phrases:

"May I be free from fear and danger."

"May I be happy."

"May I be peaceful."

Expand your awareness to sense the life of your mind, with the spectrum of experiences it can undergo—confusion, calm, agitation, serenity, contractedness, spaciousness, busyness, and stillness.

With loving kindness befriending your mind, gently repeat the phrases:

"May I be free from fear and danger."

"May I be happy."

"May I be peaceful."

Expand your awareness further to embrace the life of your heart, sensing all the joy and sorrow that can live in our hearts. Anger, love, fear, trust, anxiety, and happiness touch all of our lives. We can learn to befriend them all without exception; we can learn to embrace the world of our emotions without fear.

Continue to rest your attention in the phrases.

It is not unusual in this practice for buried feelings of confusion, pain, or anger to arise. Do not try to banish them, simply touch them with the intention to welcome them, accept them, and befriend them.

Stay with the phrases for as long as you wish. If they become an empty repetition of words, let them go for a few moments and reflect upon what it is that brings meaning, richness, and depth to your life, and upon all the qualities of heart you long to bring to fruition. Then, on the foundation of that reflection, return your attention to rest in the area of your heart and begin once more to offer the phrases of intention to yourself.

When you are ready, open your eyes and come out of your posture.

Loving Kindness for a Benefactor

Gratitude and appreciation are integral facets of loving kindness. We all depend upon one another for our well-being. Throughout our lives people have cared for us, supported and nurtured us, encouraged and inspired us. As small children our survival and well-being depended upon the love and generosity of those who cared for us. In times of struggle and conflict our ease and healing are often found through the acceptance and support of those near to us. In times of confusion, fear, and darkness, our hearts and minds are comforted and inspired by those who are able to offer gesture and words of care and loving kindness.

GUIDED MEDITATION:
LOVING KINDNESS FOR A BENEFACTOR

Begin your meditation by offering to yourself the warmth and friendliness you long for. Use the phrases of loving kindness that have
meaning for you. Keep the phrases very simple:

"May I be free from fear and danger."

"May I be happy."

"May I be peaceful."

When you feel calm and settled, invite into your heart and attention a person from the past and present who has touched your life
with their generosity without expectation of return. This benefactor
does not have to have performed some heroic act in the service of
your well-being. They may be a person who has selflessly encouraged,
supported, or inspired you. They may be someone in your family, a
friend or teacher or someone you have never met who has deeply
inspired you by their compassion, wisdom, or selflessness.

You might want to visualize that person's face, remember your
last contact with them, or simply say their name.

As you hold that person in your attention, sense the appreciation and thankfulness you feel for them.

Offer to that that person your heartfelt wishes for their happiness and well-being, silently and mindfully:

"May you be free from fear and danger."

"May you be happy."

"May you be peaceful."

As far as possible, sustain your sense of connection with the person you have chosen as you repeat the phrases.

If your attention begins to waver then come back to yourself
for a time, offering to yourself the same heartfelt wishes for your

well-being. You can let your attention alternate between your bene-factor and yourself. When other thoughts begin to flood your mind, don't judge yourself or become frustrated, just gently and calmly begin again with the phrases.

As you rest your attention firmly in the phrases you may find that a tangible sense of gratitude and appreciation arises. Let it pervade your body and heart.

Stay with the meditation as long as you are able.

When you are ready, open your eyes and come out of the posture.

GUIDED MEDITATION:
LOVING KINDNESS FOR A FRIEND

Once more relax into a calm and upright posture, closing your eyes gently.

Again bring your attention to rest in the center of your chest, in the area of your heart. Be aware of your body expanding and relaxing with each breath.

Begin your meditation once more by extending a genuine sense of loving kindness towards yourself, letting your attention rest easily within each phrase:

"May I be free from fear and danger."

"May I be happy."

"May I be peaceful."

When you are ready, invite into your heart and your attention someone who is dear to you, a friend you treasure.

Again if possible visualize their face or remember a contact you
have had with them.

As you bring them into your attention, sense the qualities of the
friendship that bonds you with that person—the trust, acceptance,
tenderness and love that you cherish.

As far as possible, sustain the connection, offering to that person
your heartfelt wishes for their well-being:

"May you be free from fear and danger."

"May you be happy."

"May you be peaceful."

Continue to rest your attention in the phrases, extending loving
kindness, warmth, and care.

If you wish you can alternate your attention between your
friend and yourself, sensing your mutual wish to be free from pain
and to be happy.

Stay present with the phrases of intention, aware of the
warmth, tenderness, and happiness that can begin to emerge in
your heart and mind. Let them pervade the whole of your body
and mind.

If your attention wanders, come gently back to the phrases, nurturing your capacity for profound loving kindness and sensitivity.

When you are ready, open your eyes and sense the calmness
and happiness that might continue to pervade your body and
mind.

Loving Kindness in the Midst of Indifference

The people we love and the people we despise both evoke powerful emotional responses in us. It is often our histories and our stories about our friends and our enemies, as much as our present relationship, that bonds us to them. Yet as we move through our lives and our days we are surrounded by countless beings with whom we share no common story or history. We walk down a crowded street, sit on a train or stand in line in a store, and all around us are those who, like us, long to be happy and free from pain. Yet we often feel neutral towards these people; we feel separate and apart from them. We easily sink into feeling indifferent towards them. They become invisible to us.

Indifference is the first building block of passivity and disconnection. A homeless man once said that the greatest curse of homelessness was not the obvious lack of a home or security—it was that most people would not look him in the eye. No matter our history, identity, race, or circumstances, we are all connected in our longing for happiness, intimacy, safety, and peace. We share the common bonds of yearning to be free from pain, turmoil, confusion, and fear. No one wants to suffer. All of us wish to be happy. Loving kindness meditation roots itself in the mutuality of these longings—it is where we are all connected.

Loving kindness meditation can bring a renewed depth to our relationships of care and intimacy. It can heal the wounds of fractured and painful relationships. On a deeper level it can awaken our hearts so that no one is dismissed or felt to be separate from ourselves. Cultivating loving kindness, we learn to embrace everyone who comes into our life with respect, sensitivity, and friendliness.

In focusing loving kindness upon a neutral person, we learn to cultivate an unconditional friendliness that has no expectation of anything in return. We are nurturing a profound inner generosity that can freely offer warmth and care without investment in result or preference. We discover that our capacity to bring caring attention to all the people we encounter in our lives lifts our hearts and forms bonds of connection and care that are rooted in sensitivity and generosity.

It is a fascinating exploration to go into each day of our life with the intention to receive each person we meet with unconditional warmth and friendliness. Cultivating the intention to ignore no one, to dismiss no one, awakens our hearts and brings only joy. When our words and actions are born of loving attention, our hearts become saturated with friendliness. There are countless opportunities for us to experiment with cultivating loving kindness for the neutral person, and a single word or gesture of care and friendliness can transform our day. Indifference turns to affection, distance turns to warmth and separation turns to connection. Cultivating loving kindness is learning to smile upon our world.

GUIDED MEDITATION:
LOVING KINDNESS IN THE MIDST OF INDIFFERENCE

Settle your body into a posture of alertness and ease.

Gently close your eyes and rest your attention in the center of your chest, in the area of your heart.

Bring a sensitive attention to your breathing. Be aware of your body expanding and relaxing with each breath.

With each out-breath consciously release anything that is pre-occupying your mind—thoughts of the past, the future, and anything you are anxious about in the present.

Begin your meditation by inviting into your attention a person you feel affection and tenderness for—a good friend or loved one.

Visualize their face or remember your last contact with them.

Offer to that person your heartfelt wishes for their well-being, using the same phrases you previously used:

"May you be free from fear and danger."

"May you be happy."

"May you be peaceful."

Sense the warmth and friendliness that may arise. Continue for some minutes to rest your attention in the phrases of intention.

Now expand your attention and bring to mind a person you feel quite neutral towards. It may be someone you work with, the teller in your bank, the driver of your bus, a person in your neighborhood you frequently pass yet do not know. If possible remember their face or the last time you encountered them.

Begin to offer to them the same warmth and friendliness you feel for the person you feel most affectionate towards, using the phrases:

"May you be free from fear and danger."

"May you be happy."

"May you be peaceful."

Sustain your connection with the neutral person for as long as you are able, with your attention steadily rooted in the phrases of intention. Don't anticipate the arising of any particular emotional responses.

If your attention begins to waver, return your focus to the person you feel more close to for a time.

When you are ready once more, switch back to the neutral person, remembering the phrases:

"May you be free from fear and danger."

"May you be happy."

> "May you be peaceful."
>
> Sense whether it is possible for you to offer the same depth of warmth and care to the neutral person as to the person who is dear to you.
>
> When you are ready, open your eyes and come out of the posture.

Loving kindness meditation can be cultivated and deepened in formal meditation practice; it can also be nurtured in all the moments of our lives. Experiment with this practice in the situations and circumstances where you feel the most separate and isolated from others. Sense the aliveness and vitality it brings.

Loving Kindness in the Face of Difficulty and Fear

The greatest challenge we face in our lives is learning to be present and receptive to those we fear or dislike. Yet the most direct way to transformation is to turn towards the moments and people in our lives we resist most strongly.

We can be deeply hurt and shattered by the words and actions of another. Even when that pain lies in a distant past we carry its scars and we can become a prisoner of it. When we are hurt by or afraid of another person, our tendency is to strike out in anger or to disconnect through fear. But it is not difficult for us to see that anger is not healed by anger and that ever-deepening division and conflict are the children of fear.

We think a lot about the people we dislike and fear in our lives. They can govern our hearts and minds. Cultivating loving kindness for these people does not mean trying to force an artificial affection or tenderness. We do, however, discover that our capacity to turn towards the people we habitually recoil from begins to loosen the grip of aversion and fear. We may, through loving kindness meditation, begin to find a way to calm the turmoil and anxiety in our own hearts and minds. We may begin to discover the possibility of greater forgiveness, tolerance, and patience.

The difficult person sometimes lives within our own hearts and minds in our relationship to ourselves. We see inner tendencies of judgment, harshness, blame, or anger that damage our well-being and impair our capacity to live with happiness and peace. We can learn to approach those areas of inner struggle with care and sensitivity and heal that inner division.

As you approach dimensions of your life where there is estrangement and struggle, whether inner or outer, take care not to expect some immediate transformation or inner emotional shift. Be patient—it is enough to find the willingness to embrace with kind attention any area of your life that has previously been banished from your heart.

GUIDED MEDITATION:
LOVING KINDNESS IN THE FACE OF DIFFICULTY AND FEAR

Find a posture for your body that is as relaxed and tension free as possible.

Gently close your eyes and bring your attention once more to rest in the center of your chest.

Remain present with your breathing for a few moments to let your mind and body settle in the present.

Begin to offer the phrases and intentions of loving kindness first to yourself:

"May I be free from fear and danger."

"May I be happy."

"May I be peaceful."

Extend your attention and invite into your heart and mind the image or awareness of someone you have had difficulty with. Let them rest in the center of your attention.

Offer them a genuine wish for their well-being and peace:

"May you too be free from fear and danger."

"May you too be happy."

"May you too be peaceful."

If it is difficult to stay connected, bring your attention once more back to yourself for a time and then open again to the difficult person, using whatever phrases have meaning for you.

You may wish to focus your phrases and intentions upon parts of your own emotional or psychological being that bring pain or harm to yourself.

Find just a few phrases that embody your wish for healing and peace:

"May I find acceptance."

"May I find peace."

"May I find healing."

After some time you may want to expand your attention to embrace all beings in our world—the people you are close to, those you struggle with, and those you feel indifferent towards.

Open your attention even further to include all those in the world you don't know, all the animals and creatures on the Earth, in the seas and in the sky:

"May all beings be free from fear and danger."

> "May all beings be happy."
>
> "May all beings be peaceful."
>
> Let your attention rest for a time in that open warm attentiveness.
>
> When you are ready, open your eyes and come out of the posture.

Compassion

Compassion is the natural response of the awakened heart to the anguish, suffering, and pain that pervade the lives of countless people in our world. It makes no hierarchies within the world of pain—terror, hunger, sickness, and rage are received and embraced, as is the suffering of confusion, aging, loss, and loneliness. In ancient Chinese and Indian cultures compassion was often expressed as the willingness to listen to the cries of the world.

Compassion is not a device to fix suffering, however, or make it go away. It lies in our capacity to open our hearts to receive the pain and anguish we encounter in our lives without fear or resistance. Compassion is gentle in its capacity to bring a receptive, unflinching empathy and care to the pain and sorrow that cannot be altered. Yet it is also concerned with healing. It can be fierce in its commitment to bringing about the end of the causes of suffering.

Wisdom and compassion lie at the heart of all great spiritual traditions. They are at times likened to the two wings of a bird. Wisdom teaches us that there is sorrow that comes with life. Our capacity to love means that we will grieve over loss. Our bodies will age and die. Our capacity for inner clarity and balance lives side by side with our capacity to experience confusion and turmoil. There are also dimensions of pain and struggle that are not intrinsic to living but are born of misunderstanding. We try to grasp the ungraspable, deny the essential rhythm of impermanence, lose ourselves in endless wanting and resistance, and suffer. Compassion is needed wherever there is pain, sorrow, and conflict. Wisdom teaches us to understand that suffering is not always wrong. At times it can come to an end through wisdom; at times it asks to be embraced in a compassionate, receptive heart.

All of us have experienced the power of compassion in our own lives. In the moments of grief, illness, loss, and heartbreak it is often the compassionate touch of another that rescues us from despair and darkness. In those moments we do not ask for prescriptions, formulas, or pity. We are healed most of all by being listened to and held within the arms of compassion. Equally, when we are with a person who is lost in fear, pain, or sorrow, it is our capacity to reach out with compassion that heals.

None of us are exempt from sorrow; none of us are exempt from the need for compassion. Our possessions, identities, position, and roles do not protect us from life and all the changes and challenges it brings. There is a universality to the experiences of grief, illness, loss, and terror. They are times of sorrow that touch us all.

Yet we all make heroic efforts to avoid pain and sorrow in this life—efforts that at times exhaust us and reinforce fear. This habitual inclination to avoid sorrow and pain submerges our capacity to nurture a profound and transforming compassion.

All too often we feel helpless in the face of pain. At times we turn away from sorrow in fear of being overwhelmed. Yet compassion begins in our willingness to open our hearts to pain—the sorrow in our own lives and the sorrow in our world. Open-hearted, we can find the equanimity and balance that allow us to receive sorrow without being shattered.

Compassion does not require heroic actions or self-sacrifice. It simply asks us to be willing to open our hearts to the cries of the world. Our world is endangered by an unwillingness to listen deeply. Our own well-being is endangered by our tendency to turn away from pain. With compassion we learn to bring a healing presence, a receptive mind, and an open heart to all the moments of sorrow we meet. It is profoundly healing.

Compassion is a quality of heart that can be cultivated in formal meditation, yet it is not confined to formal practice. We all meet countless circumstances and moments of pain that invite a compassionate presence and connection—the media images of great deprivation, the elderly person struggling to cross a road, a child in tears, the times in our own day when we find ourselves lost in turmoil, frustration, or confusion. Every moment of hurt in this world asks for us to open our hearts, to bring a fullness of attention and care.

Compassion for Blameless Sorrow

Sorrow, loss, and pain will be part of all of our lives and at some time we will all meet people in the midst of great physical, emotional or mental pain and distress—a child with a terminal illness, a friend grieving in the midst of loss, a person whose world has been shattered by violence. We see, too, endless images of people caught in famine or desolation or brutalized by wars they do not even understand. There is suffering in this world that is blameless.

Faced with situations of severe distress, our first response is often to feel stunned. We desperately search to find the "right" words or actions, yet often feel they are inadequate. Confronted with great pain and our own feelings of helplessness, we may be tempted to withdraw to protect ourselves. Alternatively, we may be tempted to throw ourselves into a frenzy of busyness, searching for solutions that can fix the suffering we see before us. Yet there is not always a solution for a broken heart, an illness, or the unexpected losses that touch our lives.

Compassion asks us to be still in the face of immeasurable pain, not to blame or judge or try to control or fix. Blame and judgment can be mechanisms we use to console ourselves in our own despair and helplessness. The heart of compassion is willing to surrender both numbness and the desperate desire to try and control the world. With compassion we can learn to open to pain and in so doing find a deep inner steadiness that can embrace the anguish we face. We can find the empathy within ourselves to dissolve the separation between ourselves and another. We can discover a way of being awake and receptive in the face of pain without being shattered or overwhelmed.

Sometimes anguish feels bottomless. Compassion too can be bottomless. Our world and all those in it who live on a daily diet of deprivation, fear, and pain cry out for compassion. We do not need to hold grandiose thoughts of healing the world—we would break beneath the weight of that expectation—but we can commit to opening our hearts to the moments in each of our days when we meet sorrow and pain, whether in ourselves or in another.

All of us have experienced times in our lives when compassion is our immediate and natural response to suffering. At such times the walls of distance melt and we see ourselves in the eyes and life of another person. These are powerful moments of connection and healing. Compassion meditation encourages us not to look upon that heartfelt response as a random accident. We can commit ourselves to finding compassion in all the moments of our lives.

GUIDED MEDITATION:
COMPASSION FOR BLAMELESS SORROW

Find a posture that is relaxed and comfortable for your body.

Let your eyes gently close.

Take a few moments to be aware of your body, its stillness, and the life within it.

Bring your attention to rest in the center of your chest, in the area of your heart, and for a few moments be aware of your breathing.

Let your mind relax and calm.

Invite into your heart and attention the image or awareness of a person who is in the midst of great physical, emotional, or mental pain. It might be someone close to you, but it can also be someone you don't know personally.

Let the image settle in your attention. Sense the struggle and sorrow that person is living with. Reflect on their hardship, heartache, or pain.

With an open heart filled with empathy and sensitivity, offer to that person your heartfelt wishes for their healing and well-being:

"May you find healing."

"May you find peace."

Let these phrases rest in your heart and mind. If you find that you begin to become lost in despair, pity, or anxiety, just come back to your breathing for a few moments to steady your heart and mind.

You may need to find words and phrases that are appropriate to the person you are connecting with. You might use:

"May you find acceptance."

"May you find ease."

Stay with the phrases as long as you wish.

> Before coming out of the posture, extend the scope of your compassion to embrace all beings:
>
> "May all beings find healing."
>
> "May all beings find peace."

Breathing in Sorrow, Breathing out Compassion

Sometimes it can be useful to use a visualization practice as a way of awakening compassion within our hearts.

> ### GUIDED MEDITATION:
> ### BREATHING IN SORROW, BREATHING OUT COMPASSION
>
> Again, find a comfortable posture for your body and close your eyes.
>
> After taking a few moments to settle your mind and body in the present, rest your attention in the area of your heart.
>
> Bring to mind an image of someone facing great heartache, struggle, or deprivation.
>
> Sense the darkness and heaviness of their pain.
>
> Imagine yourself breathing in the darkness and density like a black cloud.
>
> As you breathe out, sense yourself breathing out the lightness of peace, solace, and healing.
>
> As far as possible, sustain your connection with the person in pain in your heart and mind.

Continue focusing on your breathing, absorbing the sorrow and breathing out compassion.

When you are ready, open your eyes and come out of the meditation.

Compassion for Those Who Cause Pain

Just as there are people in our world who are in the midst of blameless sorrow and pain, so there are also those who cause harm. Compassion is a commitment to abandoning no one in our world, to exiling no one from our hearts. It is rooted in understanding that those who cause harm equally harm themselves. They are themselves casualties of their own confusion, ignorance, and fear. We too can harm others and ourselves when our hearts and minds are clouded by turmoil and fear.

Compassion embraces not only suffering but also the causes of suffering. It asks us to see beneath the actions and words that cause pain and understand the person who performs them. This is not an invitation to passivity or to justify some of the terrible acts that scar our world. There is a fierceness in compassion that is committed to ending the causes of suffering. We all need to find the courage to say "no" to causes of pain and to do all we can to end the perpetuation of violence, anger, and pain. Pain is not healed by blame, rage, and judgment; they do much to perpetuate it. In cultivating compassion we are asked to find the willingness to release our own rage and disconnection. Then we might find the words, actions, and responses that contribute to the end of sorrow.

GUIDED MEDITATION:
COMPASSION FOR THOSE WHO CAUSE PAIN

In this meditation it is not always wise to focus on the person you are most enraged with or fearful of. It may be helpful to begin with someone you reject or judge because of their harmful actions, yet in whom you can also sense their fear and hurt. This is not an easy practice. It is rooted in the understanding that separation and disconnection are not neutral but the breeding ground of anger, mistrust, and harm. So in healing the division and alienation in our own lives we take the first steps in cultivating a compassionate heart.

Begin by settling your body into a posture of stillness and ease.

Close your eyes and bring your attention to rest in the center of your chest, the area of your heart.

Take a few mindful, calm breaths to settle your attention in the present.

First invite into your heart and attention someone for whom you feel a natural and immediate compassion. Focus your attention on a person whose pain or sorrow is blameless, a person for whom compassion comes easily.

As you hold that person in your attention and heart, sense their sorrow and struggle.

Offer to them your heartfelt wishes that they may find healing, peace, and well-being with the phrases:

"May you find peace."

"May you find ease in your sorrow."

"May you find healing."

When your mind and heart feel calm, receptive, and centered, invite into your attention someone who, through their words or actions, causes harm. They may be someone close to you or even someone you have never met, someone whom you feel judgmental towards or dismissive of. Invite them into your attention, receiving them with the same sensitivity and compassion you were able to offer to the person in the midst of blameless sorrow.

Try to let go of the story, fear, or condemnation you hold. Sense them as a person like yourself who will in this life meet fear, loss, and heartache. Sense the painfulness of their confusion, rage and alienation.

Offer to them your heartfelt wishes to be free from sorrow and confusion, to find a way to peace in their hearts:

"May you find peace in your heart."

"May you be free from sorrow and confusion."

"May you find healing."

If you find it difficult to sustain a compassionate connection with the person you fear or judge, bring your attention back to the blameless person for a few moments. Once more connect with what it feels like to receive, to embrace someone with receptivity and empathy. Sense what it means just to be present with an awake and listening heart.

When you are ready, again return your attention to the difficult person. See if it is possible for you to offer the same empathy and compassion with the words:

"May you find peace in your heart."

"May you be free from sorrow and confusion."

"May you find healing."

When you are ready, open your eyes and come out of the posture.

It is important to explore this meditation without making demands of yourself or expecting an immediate result. The gulf that separates us from others in this world can feel immense. As we approach difficult people in our practice we do so with the understanding that every person in this world, no matter how destructive, misguided, or confused, longs for loving kindness and compassion, just as we do. In finding the willingness to approach with compassion those people we are prone to reject and deny, we are taking the first steps on the path of healing.

Compassion for Yourself

Many people in this world find it easier to extend compassion to others than to receive it or to offer it to themselves. Aware of the dire and bottomless pain that pervades the lives of so many people, we may feel it is inappropriate to reflect on the pain or sorrow in our own life. We may even believe that it is self-indulgent to care for our own broken hearts, ailing bodies, or confused minds.

Compassion does not measure the worth of suffering—it is a commitment to the healing of sorrow, no matter how small or large, wherever it arises. Compassion invites us to go beyond the concepts of "right" and "wrong," "good" and "bad," "worthy" and "unworthy," and explore what it means to receive all sorrow, pain, and heartache with a compassionate presence.

If we are able to surrender our tendency to flee from pain, we discover an inner balance that is not shattered by change and loss. In our relationship to our own bodies, minds, and hearts we learn the lessons of patience, tolerance, equanimity, and receptivity. In the world of our body, mind, and heart we sense the world of all bodies, minds, and hearts—moments of joy and despair, health and illness, fear and trust. Compassion invites us to be intimate with this universal story and deeply acknowledge the essential interconnectedness and interdependence of all life. The lessons of healing we learn within our own story are the lessons we bring to our lives.

Compassion for Your Body

Health turns to illness, youth to age, strength to frailty. We can feel betrayed by our bodies, afraid of their changes and panicked by unexpected illness or pain. We need to learn the lessons of befriending our bodies, feeling at home within our bodies and bringing a compassionate presence to the times of pain, illness, and frailty we will all encounter.

We are born in our bodies, live in our bodies, and will die in our bodies. Everything we do, realize, and enact in this life we will do in our bodies. Too often we live at a distance—awake to the life of our bodies only when we are startled into wakefulness through pain or illness. We can be remarkably judgmental and fearful of our bodies. We can also learn to be present in our bodies with grace and sensitivity.

Acceptance is a facet of compassion that allows us to be present and awake in our bodies, however they are. Wisdom teaches us the compassion of letting go of our images and expectations of how our bodies "should" be. Balance and equanimity teach us to find steadiness within the changes our bodies go through instead of being shattered by them. Learning to hold our bodies in a compassionate wakefulness teaches us the lessons of respect, integrity, and care we can then extend to the life of all bodies.

GUIDED MEDITATION:
COMPASSION FOR YOUR BODY

Settle into a posture of calm relaxation and let your eyes gently close.

Be aware of your body, externally and internally.

Externally, sense the places your body connects with the ground, the touch of your clothes on your body, the air on your skin.

Inwardly, feel your breathing and all the different sensations that are apparent in your body—feelings that are pleasant, places of discomfort or tension, the endless sensations that appear, linger for a time and then fade…

Reflect on your body as it was at a time when you were strong, energetic, vital.

Sense how your body has changed and how it will continue to change. Sense how your body will age and eventually die.

Reflect on the times when your body has been healthy, flexible, and at ease.

Remember too the times when your body has been in pain, broken, or ill.

Settle your attention in your body as it is in this moment, whether at ease or stressed, relaxed or in pain.

Move your attention through your body, touching all the parts of it with a sensitive wakeful attention.

As you do so, offer your body a compassionate attention with the phrases:

"May I be at peace with my body."

"May I find healing."

"May I find ease and acceptance in the midst of pain."

> Continue to move your attention through your body, meeting any places of pain or distress with an open receptive heart. Sense how much struggle and fear you may be able to let go of in the willingness to embrace pain with compassion.
>
> When you are ready, open your eyes and come out of the posture.

Compassion for Your Mind and Heart

Gain and loss, joy and sorrow, praise and blame, success and disappointment will all touch our lives. Our hearts can sing with delight, happiness, and love, but they can also bow beneath fear, anxiety, and grief. Our minds can know moments of great clarity, calm, and simplicity, but also be lost in confusion, frustration, indecision, and chaos. Just as we learn to bring compassion to an aching, distressed body, so we are asked to learn to have the same compassion for our minds and hearts.

At times it is easier to find compassion for our bodies when they are in pain or ill than it is to bring the same warmth and care to our minds and hearts. When we find ourselves a casualty of a turbulent mind or a broken heart, we are often unforgiving and ungenerous. We tell ourselves we should be different; we are prone to blame or berate ourselves. In doing so we treat our minds and hearts as enemies, yet enemies we can never divorce ourselves from. Learning to bring compassion to the chaotic mind and the turbulent heart is the beginning of calm and healing. Just as we are invited to befriend our bodies, so we are asked to embrace our hearts and minds with compassion.

GUIDED MEDITATION:
COMPASSION FOR YOUR MIND AND HEART

Find a posture that is relaxed and alert and gently close your eyes.

Bring your attention to rest in the center of your chest.

For a few moments just be aware of the natural rhythm of your breathing.

Let your mind and body relax and settle into the present moment.

Open your attention to sense any area of pain or distress that is lingering in your heart and mind. It may be the sorrow of grief, disappointment, or despair. It may be something you have found yourself obsessing about from the past or present.

Sense in your mind and heart the tightness and contractedness that surround these areas of distress.

Bring to them a compassionate presence, not expecting anything or demanding that anything goes away.

Sense them simply as pain or sorrow that ask for compassion.

Offer to yourself your heartfelt wishes for healing and peace:

"May I find ease of heart and mind."

"May I find peace."

"May I find healing."

Let your attention rest in those compassionate intentions, making peace with the distress or pain of the moment.

When your attention drifts into the story of the pain, just return your attention to your breathing for a few moments, with each out-breath releasing the resistance and complexity.

Extend your attention to embrace all beings in this world who are in distress, pain, or sorrow:

> "May all beings find ease of heart and mind."
>
> "May all beings find peace."
>
> "May all beings find healing."
>
> When you are ready, open your eyes and come out of the posture.

Compassion in Grief and Loss

Our capacity to form bonds of intimacy with people in our lives inevitably means that all of us will experience the sorrow of loss and separation. Grief is our very human and heartfelt response to death and the endings of the relationships that have gladdened our hearts. In the midst of grieving it can feel that it will be endless, as if the fabric of our lives has been torn apart.

In the pain of grief we may find ourselves lost in a cascade of memories, replaying the endless stories of our relationship with the person who has died. Our hearts can fill with an overwhelming sense of injustice, particularly when someone we care for deeply dies unexpectedly and unpredictably. Part of our grieving in those moments may be to shut out the world, to seek for causes we may never be able to find or understand, or to blame ourselves for not preventing the death.

Grief is a territory in which we feel rootless and bereft. It can seem a time of such darkness, sorrow, and uncertainty that there is nowhere we can find a place of rest. Meditation practice is not a device to make grief disappear, but it can offer a way of discovering a sense of refuge and ease. We can learn to find a home for ourselves in the present, one moment at a time, rather than being lost in stories of the past or fears about the future. Grief has no predetermined timetable, but within it we can discover a way of caring for ourselves.

The times of greatest sorrow in our lives are the times that ask for the greatest compassion. Compassion has its roots in listening, the capacity to receive sorrow without fear or anxiety. In grief, being listened to by others is part of our healing. Our capacity to listen deeply to our own hearts and minds is equally part of the fabric of our healing.

GUIDED MEDITATION: COMPASSION IN GRIEF AND LOSS

Take a few moments to settle into a posture that is relaxed and comfortable as possible.

Gently close your eyes and be aware of your whole body.

Let your breathing relax. Consciously take a few slightly fuller breaths, and as you breathe out, be aware of releasing the out-breath fully.

With each out-breath sense your body relaxing more and more deeply.

Bring your attention to your heart area, the center of your chest, and sense what sensations or feelings are being held in that area of your body.

Your heart may feel heavy, contracted, or painful. Let your attention rest gently there without demanding that it should feel different.

Offer to yourself heartfelt compassion and care:

"May I find ease within this sorrow."

"May I find peace within this sorrow."

"May I find healing."

> Thought and memories may flood your mind, bringing their own waves of grief. Embrace them with the same compassionate attention. Discover that it is possible to be present with these thoughts and memories without becoming lost.
>
> Bring your attention gently back to the phrases of compassion:
>
> "May I find ease within this sorrow."
>
> "May I find peace within this sorrow."
>
> "May I find healing."
>
> Stay with this practice as long as it is comfortable for you. In the moments of greatest heartache you may discover that it is possible for you to find some sense of refuge and ease within the phrases of compassion.

Altruistic Joy

An antidote to feelings of unhappiness and inner deprivation is finding the generosity of heart that is able to appreciate and celebrate the blessings in our own lives. And the great generosity that is able to celebrate the happiness of other people is a powerful antidote to the damaging feelings of envy, resentment, and comparison that scar our spirit.

Cultivating gladness in the happiness of others and in our own lives relieves much of the alienation, darkness, and estrangement that can shadow our lives. Celebrating blessings counters the powerful tendencies that lead us to feel we are either caught in endless competition with other people or need to prove our worth to ourselves.

So much unhappiness is born of resentment, comparison of ourselves with others, jealousy, and the belief that our happiness relies upon what we have yet to gain, achieve, and accumulate. We can be locked within a world of bitterness and envy to the extent that we ignore the ease and happiness available to us.

Appreciation illuminates the moments of love, happiness, and ease that are part of all of our lives. It is not a denial of unhappiness, sorrow or loss, but it teaches us to hold the moments of sorrow in our lives in a more spacious and loving way.

A DAILY PRACTICE:
APPRECIATION

Sense the places in your life where your heart begins to contract with envy, resentment, or judgment. Perhaps you support a sports team who loses against a rival team. Can you celebrate their delight in their win, appreciate their skills and their happiness? Perhaps you hear someone speak of an exhilarating inner experience they've had. Can you celebrate their delight rather than being lost in envy? A friend succeeds in winning a job you coveted. Can you celebrate their happiness with them rather than contracting in envy?

Take some moments to reflect upon the blessings in your own life—having a healthy body, or even the inner balance to embrace ill health without fear, having enough to eat, shelter, life itself. Reflect on those people who care for and love you, those who are attentive to your needs and who support you. Reflect on being able to live a life not overshadowed by deprivation, terror, or violence.

Take some moments to reflect on your own capacity to care for others, to attend to their needs and to find compassion and generosity in your own heart.

Sense deeply the places of ease and happiness that are woven within the fabric of your life. Let appreciation fill your heart and mind.

GUIDED MEDITATION:
ALTRUISTIC JOY

Let your body settle into a posture of ease and balance.

Gently close your eyes and settle your attention in your body and in the present moment.

Invite into your attention a friend who is happy or joyous. They may be delighting in the birth of a child, in recovered health after a spate of illness or in a life event that has brought a newfound happiness.

Sense their gladness, gratefulness, or delight as you have seen it in them.

Offer them a generous wish that their happiness may deepen and continue.

Find a few simple words or phrases that express the generosity of heart you feel for them:

"May your happiness deepen."

"May your life continue to bring gladness and delight."

Next invite into your attention someone whom you envy or feel some resentment towards because of the happiness they are experiencing. It may be a friend, a colleague or even someone do not know but whom you admire and yet at the same time envy.

Offer to that person a generosity of heart that rejoices in their gladness, accomplishments, or successes:

"May your happiness deepen."

"May your gladness continue."

Sense whether it is possible to offer that same generosity of altruistic joy to yourself. Take some moments to reflect on the many blessings and moments of happiness and ease that are present in your life in this moment. Reflect on your capacity for love, care and empathy, on the people in your life who care for you, on the moments of gladness and delight you encounter. Say to yourself:

"May I deepen in happiness and generosity."

"May I live with appreciation and gladness."

When you are ready, open your eyes and come out of the posture.

Cultivating Fearlessness: Exploring Fear

Fear is one of the most debilitating and paralyzing emotions in our lives. It is often the root of a wide spectrum of other emotions in our lives. Fear appears in various forms, from twinges of anxiety to waves of terror and dread that obstruct our capacity to live with openness and receptivity. It appears in the forms of self-consciousness, mistrust, and doubt. Increasingly we begin to see that fear thrives in a lack of awareness.

Cultivating fearlessness does not presume that fear will never arise in our hearts and lives. Fearlessness is not living without fear, but turning directly towards the fears and anxieties that do arise. When we are willing to do this, we learn that it is possible to embrace fear with a gentle and loving attention rather than being governed by it. We learn to touch fear with compassion, to investigate and understand it.

GUIDED MEDITATION:
EXPLORING FEAR

Sit comfortably and allow your body to relax fully. Bring a gentle attention to any places in your body where there is tightness or discomfort. Gently and consciously soften those areas, allowing your whole body to relax.

Close your eyes and for a few moments pay attention to your breathing. Give particular attention to your outgoing breath. With each out-breath, relax more deeply and consciously release any of the turmoil or busyness in your mind. Follow each out-breath with your attention until its very end.

When you feel calmer, consciously invite into your attention and heart something that makes you afraid. Initially, don't focus upon anything you feel terrified or overwhelmed by, but upon a dimension of your life that you may habitually flinch from or avoid. It might be a fear of speaking honestly, a difficult person who is part of your life, making changes or relationships you tend to turn away from. It may be a fear of illness, aging, or death. It might be a fear of the dark or of loss.

Let yourself feel the fear that arises in the face of the object, situation, or event you resist or feel anxious about.

Sense where the fear is in your body and explore those sensations with your attention. Cultivate a curious attention, sensing how the sensations change and move.

Allow yourself to rest within those sensations. If they become overwhelming, come back to your breathing for a few moments, connect deeply with each out-breath and allow your mind and body to calm once more.

As you invite the object or situation of anxiety into your attention, be aware of the different emotions, memories, or images that arise. Let them rest in your attention without trying to get rid of them or becoming lost within them. They may be uncomfortable, but you may also begin to sense they are not intrinsically threatening.

Sense that fear and all its associated images and reactions may be uncomfortable yet in itself need not be threatening or overwhelming.

Move your attention back and forth between the fear and your breathing, cultivating a calm steadiness moment to moment.

Sense the way that avoidance deepens and perpetuates fear.

Sense too how fear diminishes in the light of calm attention.

Throughout the meditation continue to check in with your body, relaxing and softening any tightness or tension that appears.

When you are ready, open your eyes and come out of the posture.

Understanding Anger

Personally and universally, we are aware of the devastating effects of anger and the harm it brings. Alienation, fear, violence, and pain are its inevitable offspring. Anger appears in the moments of aversion that lead us to banish people from our hearts; it appears too in the violence and aggression that wound countless lives.

Anger is one of the most difficult of emotions to be truly conscious and aware of within. Often it appears as an almost unstoppable wave that erupts in our words and actions. Then we carry its residues in the form of regret and guilt. Yet we can learn to be aware of anger, understand it, befriend it and heal the fear and hurt that are both its cause and its result.

Awareness does not demand an emotional neutrality, but an ever-deepening sensitivity to the world around us and within us. Anger can be an awakening energy that can motivate us to question the causes of harm and find in ourselves the commitment to bringing about the end of those causes. This is anger held in the light of awareness, anger that inspires healing, understanding, and discriminating wisdom and action.

GUIDED MEDITATION: UNDERSTANDING ANGER

Settle into a posture of ease and balance, being upright and alert yet also fully relaxed.

Gently close your eyes.

Begin your meditation with a few minutes of loving kindness for all beings.

Use a few simple phrases that embody a sense of unconditional warmth and friendliness:

"May all beings be free from fear and danger."

"May all beings be happy."

"May all beings be peaceful."

Let your attention rest gently in those phrases, sensing the myriad of beings in this world who share the longing to be safe, loved, and happy.

Gently invite into your attention someone with whom you are angry or an event that provokes anger within you.

Sense what arises in your body, heart, and mind as your focus on that person or event.

Sense what anger feels like, emotionally and physically, and allow yourself to feel those sensations fully without judging or condemning them.

Many thoughts, memories, or images may appear. Just bring a sensitive attention to them without becoming lost.

Come back to your body, consciously softening any part of it that begins to tighten.

Be aware of attempts to justify or explain your anger or aversion, then let the thoughts go and come back to focus on the person or event that disturbs or challenges you.

Sense whether it is possible to stay with that focus, not avoiding it or flinching from it.

Reflect on what might be needed for you to connect more fully with the person you are angry with or to bring a steadiness of heart to the situation that enrages you.

Can you find the openness of heart to accept your own anger and find the inner spaciousness where it does not overwhelm you?

Can you find the openness of heart and inner balance to meet the event that angers you without creating more harm or division?

Be willing to know anger deeply and fully—to be present and awake within it.

Ask yourself where the healing might begin and what words or acts would support that healing.

Come back to the phrases of loving kindness for a few moments.

When you are ready, open your eyes and come out of the posture.

CHAPTER 4

A Mind of Wisdom

Our minds are the forerunners of our speech, actions, choices, and the way that we personally experience and interpret the world. They can be a cauldron of seething thoughts, worries, memories and plans. They can also be pervaded by profound serenity, stillness, and clarity. The times of greatest confusion, obsession, turmoil, and preoccupation are all experienced within our minds. But our minds also have the capacity to be a landscape of clarity, simplicity, and peace.

Learning to care for our minds with sensitivity, understanding, and mindfulness, we learn to care for everything that is born of our minds. A mind rooted in calm clarity, understanding, and stillness finds its embodiment in every word, gesture, and choice in our lives. Learning to befriend our minds, we discover the possibility of finding ease in every area of our lives.

When our minds are overly full, burdened with unnecessary thought and preoccupation, they propel us through our lives with haste and agitation. Learning to find spaciousness within our minds, we approach our world with a deepening care and calmness.

A central part of meditation practice is devoted to understanding the nature of our minds, simply because they play such a central role in our lives and our capacity to find well-being. It is possible to embrace our minds with awareness—to sense on a moment-to-moment level the arising and passing of thoughts, images, and mental states. Our minds are no obstacle to deep understanding and compassion—the obstacle lies in the unconsciousness or lack of awareness that leads us to be lost in clouds of confusion. In meditation we explore the possibility of bringing a sensitive and clear attentiveness to our minds, just as we learn to bring that quality of attention to every other dimension of our lives.

Knowing Your Mind

In the times of greatest inner chaos and turmoil in our lives we can regard our minds almost as enemies—untrustworthy and the source of pain. There are moments when our deepest and most noble intentions to cultivate loving kindness, generosity, and openness seem to be sabotaged by the compelling and habitual thoughts and fears that take root in our minds. Unpredictability appears to be part of our minds. Moments of calm and peace are overtaken by bursts of preoccupation and obsession. The wonderful moments of serenity and ease we nurture are suddenly ambushed by frantic bursts of anxiety or rehearsals of the future. The state and quality of our minds often seems to be beyond our control. We wish to be present, spacious, and clear, only to find ourselves floundering in dullness or clouds of confusion.

It is tempting to blame our minds for the turmoil and agitation we can all too easily find ourselves lost in. But the first step in developing clarity of mind is to let go of the blame and begin to approach our minds with interest, investigation, and sensitivity.

Meditation is not anti-thought, nor is it a means to suppress the mind. Just as the mind can be the source of some of the most destructive acts and conflicts in our world, so too can it be the source of some of the greatest insights and creativity in our world. The divisions and separations that scar our world will also be healed through our ability and willingness to find peace and understanding within our own minds.

Acknowledging the power of the mind both for chaos and stillness, we learn to bring a meditative awareness directly to our own minds and all their activities. We learn we can find simplicity and cultivate the capacity of our minds for insight, investigation, and stillness. We discover we can see thought just as thought, held within the same rhythm of arising and passing as everything else in our lives. We can think with clarity, learn to investigate the places of confusion that beleaguer us, and nurture a mind of peace.

A calm mind is not intrinsically a mind that it is devoid of thought. If meditative depth were dependent upon the absence of thought, it would be irrelevant to our lives. Learning to investigate and understand our minds, we enhance our capacity to think and reflect with clarity. We discover the wisdom of releasing much of the identification and holding that agitates our minds. We learn to let go of many of the futile avenues of thinking, judgment, anxiety, and obsession that do not contribute to our well-being. A mind that is deeply rooted in calmness is an ally in our lives, the source of effective, clear action.

Approaching our minds in a meditative way, on a moment-to-moment level, we see more clearly the impact of the mind upon our bodies, hearts, and all of the relationships we form in our lives. Too often we are so entangled in the stories we hold about ourselves and the world that we forget how to listen with openness and sensitivity. Meditation teaches us to listen to our minds, to reject nothing and to discover the freedom of not being entangled and lost in the world of interpretation and judgment.

The first step in the cultivation of a mind of serenity and wisdom is to learn to be aware of our minds, moment to moment. Awareness is the forerunner of all transformation. It is what illuminates the mind, bringing clarity into a dimension of our lives that often seems to be shrouded in clouds of confusion and complexity. In meditation we bring a clear, sensitive attention directly to all of the activities of our minds.

Noting

The first step in cultivating a mind of calmness and clarity is to know the nature of our mind on a moment-to-moment level, to cultivate a mindful intimacy with it, exploring it in all its movements and activities.

We discover that our mind is not a static, uninterrupted entity. It is an ongoing process of arising and passing thoughts, images, memories, plans, moods, and responses. We receive the world, moment to moment, through our sensory doors, and our minds perceive and interpret those impressions. The inner world of association, memory, comparison, emotion, and evaluation is set in motion.

It is helpful to see the changing nature of our mental processes, as it is the first step in forming a mindful relationship to our minds. As we learn to be increasingly present within those mental processes we discover we are not helpless, not sentenced to an eternal inner life of floundering, reactivity, and powerlessness before the force of our minds. We are able to introduce into the life of our minds the qualities of investigation, serenity, and simplicity. These are the qualities that teach us how to let go of confusion and complexity and realize the capacity of our minds for clarity, understanding, and creativity.

We discover, too, that the mind is not always constant—that the space and stillness between thoughts can learn to sense the arising of thoughts and be increasingly attuned to some of the states of mind that can, if unnoticed, govern our relationship to every moment in our life.

If our minds are at peace, we discover increasing depths of peace everywhere in our lives. If our minds are balanced and receptive, we are no longer prone to being lost in the multiplicity of events that are part of all of our lives. Being intimate with our own minds enhances our capacity to understand the nature of all minds. Learning to step out of the cycles of reactivity and confusion within ourselves, we discover the means to bring clarity and sensitivity to each moment.

GUIDED MEDITATION:
NOTING

Find a posture in which your body can be relaxed and upright. Take a few moments to settle into that posture, finding a deep sense of ease within your body.

Let your eyes gently close.

Bring your attention to rest within your breathing, focusing your attention either on the area of your upper lip and nostrils or on the rising and falling of your abdomen with each breath.

Let your attention rest lightly in that area of your body, cultivating a base of calm attentiveness.

As you rest your attention in your breathing, begin to sense all the moments when your attention is drawn to whatever is occurring in your mind.

Fantasy, memory, planning, judgment, daydreaming, rehearsing— make a simple note of whatever is occurring so you can see clearly where your attention is lingering in the world of thought.

Note it calmly, clearly, and then return your attention to your breathing.

You may find that you are present only with a single breath before your attention is attracted once more to activity in your mind. Just breathe that breath fully, sensing its beginning and its ending.

If your attention is once more drawn to a thought or series of thoughts or images that have appeared in your mind, again just make a simple mental note of that activity. Thinking, daydreaming, planning, fantasy, memory—as far as you are able, just note each thought simply and clearly.

Return once more to the next breath. Sense that each time you return your attention to your breathing that you are letting go of complexity and entanglement.

There may be moments when you are not aware of the movement of your attention from your breath and into a thought pattern. Suddenly you wake up as if from a dream, realizing you have been lost in a thought or fantasy. Don't judge those moments, just make a simple mental note—"Thinking, thinking'—and return to the next breath.

Don't be tempted to try to figure out where the thoughts are coming from or what underlies them. Just bring simplicity into the world of thought and imagery, cultivating calmness and clarity with that simplicity.

Let your breath be an anchor and also be a mirror, reflecting all those moments when your attention leaves your breath and goes to your mind.

Know when your attention is present within your breathing and when your attention is present within thought. Be equally attentive, with calmness and sensitivity, to each of those moments.

You may discover that when you bring a conscious attention to a thought, the thought simply dissolves and disappears. This is fine —don't try to hold on to anything. Sense the disappearing of the thought and again bring a wholehearted attentiveness to your breathing.

Sense the possibility of seeing a thought as a thought, arising and passing, appearing and fading away.

Sense a breath as a breath, arising and passing, appearing and fading away.

Let yourself rest in calm attentiveness, aware and clear within the life of your mind.

As your attention deepens, you may discover that your thought processes begin to calm and slow down. You may sense a growing capacity to see thoughts more clearly and realize that you are closer to the moments when thought processes begin to appear in your mind. You may discover a growing stillness that does not rely upon the absence of thought but is tangible within the presence of thought.

Patiently cultivate your capacity to be aware of the life of your mind. You may encounter many moments of becoming lost or entranced in thought. Always be willing to begin again, reconnecting with your breath and the moment you are in.

Cultivate calmness and clarity of mind in each moment.

When you are ready, open your eyes and come out of the posture.

Thought

As you become more intimate with the nature of your mind it will become apparent there are several different layers of thought. It is as if giving attention to the mind allows the release of the multiple impressions we have accumulated. Giving attention to what it happening in your mind is a direct way of letting go of some of this accumulation, which if unattended to tends simply to clutter the spaciousness of mind possible for us.

Some of the thoughts that appear will be fleeting and random. Momentary memories and images will arise and pass. They carry no particular underlying messages or emotional charge.

We can see too that there are levels of thought that offer a strange entertainment value. In moments when we feel bored or discontented, the tendency of the mind to find something to occupy itself with is highlighted. Fantasies, daydreams, speculative thoughts about the future, and even painful mental creations suddenly become magnetic. This level of thought becomes a way of comforting or consoling ourselves in moments of unease. But rarely does being lost in "entertainment" thinking lead to greater clarity and calmness of being. More frequently it serves to agitate the mind and leads us to lose ourselves in a mentally constructed world, disconnected from the moment.

There are also levels of thought that are insistent and repetitive. Painful memories, images, conversations, and events replay themselves over and over. Anxiety-driven thoughts about the future visit repetitively and we find ourselves trying to guarantee a future that is free from challenge or distress. Judgmental thoughts about ourselves or others insert themselves into our attention again and again, with each visit triggering familiar feelings of blame, unworthiness, or anger. The stories within this realm of repetitive thinking are familiar to us—we have found ourselves lost in the same thoughts and feelings a thousand times before—yet they seem to have a powerful grip on our minds and hearts. Lost in our stories and repetitive thinking, we find our confidence in our capacity to find clarity and spaciousness is sabotaged.

We see too within our minds the capacity to reflect, inquire, and investigate. There are levels of thought that are creative, that inquire into what we don't know, that give birth to new ventures and bring new understandings into our lives. We see that our thoughts are a vehicle for articulating insight and giving form to intuition. These are thoughts that contribute to enlivening and awakening us.

Increasingly in meditation we attune ourselves to the different layers of thought that appear, sensing what contributes to clarity, depth, and well-being and what undermines it. Unattended to, thought creates a debilitating mental indigestion. With sensitivity and mindful attention, we discover it is possible to use it wisely.

GUIDED MEDITATION:
THOUGHT

Settle into a posture of ease and balance. Let your body be upright and alert yet also deeply at ease.

Let your eyes gently close and take a few moments to allow your body to settle into a calm stillness.

For a few moments bring your attention just to listening. Sense the sounds that are near and distant. Be aware of the changes in all the sounds you hear, their appearing and their fading. Sense the silence that is present between the sounds.

Be fully focused and attentive in the moment, calming your mind and body.

Bring your attention to be fully aware of what is happening in your mind in the moment.

Be aware of the thoughts that are present. As far as you are able, sense the different layers of thought that arise and pass.

Notice the brief appearance of images or thoughts that arise and disappear of their own accord—fleeting memories, plans that appear only for a moment and then dissolve.

Sense the moments when you find yourself consciously or unconsciously spinning thought patterns to keep yourself occupied. Notice perhaps the desire to be busy, to have something to think about, dwell upon, or be enlivened by.

Sense the possibility of sustaining a clarity and simplicity of attention in those moments.

Bring your attention back to listening, being fully present with the sounds that are available to you. For a few moments, rest within the receptivity of just listening.

Bring your attention once more to what is happening in your mind. What has happened to the thoughts or images that only moments ago seemed so entrancing? They may simply have disappeared or been replaced by a new stream of thought.

Sense the moments when your attention is drawn into more repetitive, insistent thoughts that you have thought a thousand times before.

Instead of being lost in the familiar stories, bring your attention to your body. Sense whether those more entrenched thought patterns are making an impact on your body.

Do you notice the rhythm of your breathing alter in the face of those thoughts? Does it become tighter or more contracted?

Do you notice uncomfortable or painful sensations arising in your chest, back, or abdomen with the thoughts? Are there ways in which your body begins to tighten or tense?

Let your attention rest fully in your body rather than being lost in the thoughts. Explore what is happening in your body with a sensitive attention.

When you feel balanced and clear in your connection with your body, bring your attention back to your mind and the insistent thoughts.

See if you are able to sense the emotional foundation of those repetitive stories and thoughts. Is it sadness, anger, regret, anxiety? As far as possible, sense that fully. Many of our insistent thoughts are emotionally charged—they are asking for understanding and attention.

Let your attention move between awareness of what is happening in your body and awareness of what is happening in your mind. Whenever you begin to be lost in the stories, come back to being as fully attentive as possible in your body.

Try not to attempt to explain, justify, or analyze the emotional foundations of the thoughts that appear—this becomes another story. Use your attention to cultivate the clarity and spaciousness that allow a more direct intuition to arise.

Notice the moments when the thoughts are more reflective and insightful. Sense the simplicity that is part of the fabric of these thoughts—they appear, last for a time, and fade away.

Experiment with bringing your attention directly to thought. Sense the possibility of cultivating profound clarity, simplicity, and stillness even in the midst of thought.

Let yourself know your mind deeply, understanding its potential for creativity, reflection, and calm investigation.

When you are ready, open your eyes and come out of the posture.

States of Mind

Each moment in our lives our response to ourselves and to the world is shaped and formed by the state of our mind. Mental states are the moods or climate of mind that lie beneath our thoughts, words, and responses. Dullness, clarity, restlessness, anxiety, depression, elation, anxiety, and spaciousness are all states of mind.

States of mind can change with extraordinary frequency and unpredictability throughout our day. The calmness present at breakfast can be lost in the agitation in which we find ourselves at lunch. Excitement turns to apprehension, elation to sadness, contractedness to spaciousness.

Our state of mind is clearly the parent of all our words, thoughts, and actions. An agitated mind gives birth to agitated reactions. A mind of calmness and clarity finds its expression in thoughts and acts of calmness.

Meditation does not seek to cultivate the "right" state of mind or to forge a standard, static way of being in the world. It concerns itself with understanding and freedom, with discovering a way of being in the world where we are not governed by anything.

The states of mind that can so easily govern our way of being in the world are often so extraordinarily subtle that we may not even sense them. Rather than learning to recognize and judge the changing states of mind that arise and pass in each moment of our lives, we can question what leads to peace and calmness and what leads to confusion and struggle. We can learn that we can let go of the states of mind that lead us to live in a state of perpetual reactivity and cultivate those that allow us to respond wholeheartedly with generosity and serenity.

GUIDED MEDITATION:
STATES OF MIND

Settle your body into a posture of calm relaxation. Be alert and upright, embodying in your posture the qualities of attentiveness and presence that connect you to this moment and that you seek to cultivate inwardly.

Let your eyes gently close and for a few moments just be aware of your breathing, establishing your attention inwardly and in the moment.

Soften any areas of tension within your body, cultivating a deep sense of ease.

Consciously let go of thoughts of past and future and any preoccupations in the present.

Be present, where you are, in this moment.

Ask yourself what is the state of your mind right now. Is it calm, agitated, anxious, spacious, aversive, receptive?

The thoughts or images that are present are often a clue to the state of your mind. Rehearsing, repetitive planning thoughts may indicate an underlying anxiety or agitation. Repetitive thoughts or images about the past may hint at an underlying state of remorse, disappointment, anger, or sadness. If it is simply difficult to pay attention, your mind being full of random, scattered thought, it may be indicative of a state of restlessness. If it feels impossible even to be present, to sense what is happening in your mind, it may point to a state of dullness or disconnection.

Sense whether it is possible for you to notice the predominant state of your mind at the moment.

Sometimes the clues are in your body. If your body feels restless, unable to be still, you may notice a corresponding agitation in your mental state. If your body feels heavy, contracted, this too may be a clue to the state of your mind. There may be areas of uncomfortable or painful sensation in your body, indicating a mind lost in a particular mood or state, or your body may feel calm, relaxed, and spacious, which is the mental state of ease, serenity, or peace registering in your body.

As you sense the state of your mind, ask yourself whether it is conducive to your well-being and your capacity to be aware and balanced in this moment in your life.

If you sense an underlying mental state of dullness, restlessness, aversion, anxiety, or unease, ask yourself what is needed to dispel that state.

If there is dullness, it may be appropriate to cultivate a more precise, clear sense of connection with your breath or body, noticing all the changes occurring within them as ways of clearing the clouds of dullness.

If there is agitation or anxiety, it may be helpful to cultivate a more spacious attention. Bring your attention to listening or to simply being aware of the stillness of your body.

If you sense an underlying anxiety or preoccupation, it may be helpful to focus your attention on consciously letting go of the thoughts and images that arise. Renew the intention to let go each time you find yourself lost in a cascade of thinking. Bring your attention to the natural rhythm of your breathing from its beginning to its end, relaxing in that movement.

Whenever you find yourself gripped by a state of mind that does not lend itself to clarity, connectedness, or spaciousness, it is helpful to explore what is absent in that moment. Reflect on the qualities of heart and mind that would restore balance, responsiveness, and openness. Sense whether it is possible to culti-vate those qualities.

As you become more aware of the states of mind that arise and pass in your meditation you may discover that it is possible to be fully awake and present within them with acceptance and clarity. This in itself is often the beginning of changing compelling mind states. Our capacity to be aware within these states is the key that unlocks a genuine sense of freedom and deep inner balance. We see a state of mind as a state of mind, not necessarily a reliable description of the world or of ourselves. The differing states of mind that appear and fade away in our day are like different winds that we can allow to move through us. We can be receptive to them, yet not governed by them.

Spend the time of your meditation sensing the different states or moods that appear.

Remain firmly in an inner posture of steadiness, sensing the mental states without judgment. Find calmness within them.

When you are ready, open your eyes and come out of the posture.

You may find it useful to carry this awareness of the states of your mind into your day, pausing occasionally just to ask yourself: "What is the state of my mind?"

Meditative Questioning

Investigation into the nature of the mind is one of the primary keys to understanding it more deeply. In contemplating the mind it is essential that there is no underlying motive to make the mind stop or disappear. Our contemplation needs to be rooted in interest and inquiry rather than aversion. If we approach the mind with elements of judgment or aversion, it will only fuel its agitation. A benevolent interest, dedicated to understanding, is what allows us to find spaciousness and serenity within our mental world. Calmness is built on the foundations of interest, just as anxiety and agitation are built on the foundations of blame or rejection.

Being mindful of the mind is not a path of cultivating a mind that is increasingly full, but a way of learning to release the layers of superfluous thought that confuse our capacity for clarity and wisdom. Mindful investigation is not the cultivation of discursive or speculative thinking, but a calm questioning that deepens a more intuitive understanding.

GUIDED MEDITATION:
INVESTIGATION OF MIND

Settle your body into a meditative posture—upright, alert, and relaxed.

Let your eyes gently close.

Be aware of your body, externally and internally.

Sense the points where your body contacts the ground, cushion, or chair, and the pressure or warmth at those points of contact.

Sense the inner life of your body—the movement of your breath and your body's response to each in-breath and out-breath. Sense the different sensations that are apparent within your body. Bring a gentle and clear attention to those bodily sensations as they arise and pass.

Now expand your attention to be aware of your whole body, sensing its stillness and balance.

Let yourself settle deeply into that stillness and bodily awareness.

Now bring your attention to be aware of your mind just as it is in this moment.

Sense the different thoughts and images that come and go without lingering in any of them.

Be aware of how some of those thoughts and images make only a momentary appearance and then disappear, to be replaced by another thought or image.

Sense how some of the thoughts or images linger, taking a more predominant or lasting place in your mind.

Notice the attraction or aversion that may arise in response to these thoughts.

Bring a calm and simple question to those thoughts or images that have taken root in your mind: "What is this?"

Let your attention rest in this question without expecting any particular answer.

As you apply the question to the thoughts or images you may sense that it has the effect of dissolving them.

Keep your attention firmly rooted in the question. Whenever your mind is drawn into more discursive thought or begins to wander, calmly and gently bring your attention back to the question once more. See the wandering just as it is: the tendency to become preoccupied or to demand an answer.

The question "What is this?" brought to thought simply allows it to be seen more fully and clearly. Let it be the base and anchor for your attention. Let it illuminate your mind, revealing both its activities and the spaciousness within it. As your meditation deepens, the question will rest more and more naturally at the forefront of your consciousness—a key to depth and understanding.

It is important that the question does not become mechanical or habitual, but is a genuine inquiry into the moment. The question is not asked in search of an answer but in search of connectedness and understanding.

Whenever your attention strays, explore the possibility of bringing the question also to those moments of wandering or being lost. Ask them: "What is this?"

When you are ready, open your eyes and come out of the meditation.

You may wish to explore this pathway of simple questioning not only in formal meditation but also in all the moments in your day when you find yourself lost in confusion, inattention, or complexity. Ask simply: "What is this?"

Letting Go

Life continues to teach us the direct relationship between peace and our willingness to let go. No matter how tightly or fearfully we hold on to something, inwardly and outwardly, it will change and we will be asked to let it go. The art of being able to let go fully and freely in every moment of our lives is the art of finding balance and serenity.

Fear makes us hold tightly to countless things in our lives; trust and understanding teach us how to let go. The openness and intimacy we long to find in all of our relationships are born of our capacity to let go of mistrust, anger, and alienation. Our capacity to be fully present in all of the moments of our lives, to be touched and taught by them, is born of our willingness to let go of our preoccupations with past and future.

Learning to let go will never be born of willpower, forcing, or striving. Commanding ourselves to let go will only set up new standards and judgments of success and failure that harm our well-being. Letting go is born of calmness, compassion, and understanding. These are qualities we cultivate moment to moment in our meditation practice and our lives. Every time we sit in meditation may be a time when we are asked to let go a thousand times. Each day of our lives invites us to let go in countless moments and encounters.

We learn to let go not in order to make ourselves suffer, feel deprived, or bereft, but to bring about an end to suffering, to feelings of deprivation and fear. Letting go is the art of happiness and contentment, cultivated moment to moment.

Finding a greater simplicity in our lives has the inevitable companion of learning to let go. As we become increasingly sensitive to our inner life we begin to see the ways in which we are imprisoned by whatever it is we are clinging to most tightly. The times when we feel least free, connected, and open in our lives are the times when we are desperately trying to make life conform to our wishes and expectations. At these times we are lost in identification and holding. The times of greatest freedom are the times when we can embrace each moment, person, and encounter in our lives just as it is, free of demand and expectation.

Meditation practice invites us to bring a wholehearted attention to all the places where we struggle and suffer most deeply.

We often discover that these are the places where we are holding on most tightly. Opinions, expectations, roles, identities, fears, objects, goals, and desires are all fertile ground for holding and clinging, so becoming the places of greatest distress in our lives. Yet it is in the places where we hold on most fiercely that we can also discover the greatest freedom as we learn to loosen the hold of clinging.

It is not always difficult for us to see the places in our lives that are inviting us to learn to let go, but there are many ways in which we learn to let go freely and wholeheartedly. Whatever way we learn is to be honored—it is in the service of peace. When our mind is calm and attentive, letting go is often effortless and easeful. And the more we are able to let go, the more generosity, compassion, simplicity, and freedom we discover in our lives.

GUIDED MEDITATION:
LETTING GO

Let your body relax into an alert and upright meditative posture.

Gently close your eyes.

Focus your attention for some moments on your breathing, consciously following each out-breath with your attention until its very ending.

Sense the letting go within your breathing—letting go of preoccupation, busyness, and turmoil.

Settle into calmness and simplicity, being fully present in just this moment.

When you find yourself present and calm in your breathing, open your attention and invite into your attention the most recent

---

memory of a moment, an event, or conversation that was burdened by struggle, anxiety, or resistance.

Hold that memory or image gently and calmly in your attention, without being tempted to justify, condemn, or explain it.

Ask yourself what it is you may be being asked to let go of to find greater ease, peace, and simplicity. Is it expectation, judgment, fear, anger?

Hold the question gently in your attention and sense the response that may intuitively arise from your heart.

If you find yourself becoming lost in the story, return your attention to your breathing for a few moments, releasing each out-breath fully, until once more you find yourself calm and relaxed.

You might invite into your attention another recent time when you have been embroiled in confusion, argument, or discord with another person.

Again hold that image or moment simply in your attention.

What are you being asked to let go of, to release to bring the disharmony or argument to an end?

Sense how you may walk down familiar pathways of judgment, blame, or self-hatred. Is it possible to bring some wise restraint to those pathways, to walk new pathways of compassion, tenderness, and loving kindness?

Whenever your attention gets caught in a memory of story, return to be aware of your breathing.

Sense that your willingness to come back to your breath, to be fully present in just one breath and one moment at a time, is in itself a way of letting go. It is releasing the story and the sense of imprisonment.

Hold lightly in your attention the question: "What can I let go of to find greater simplicity, peace, and freedom in my life?"

Allow an intuitive response to emerge, sensing the spaciousness born of being able to let go.

When you are ready, open your eyes and come out of the meditation.

Who Am I?

There are a number of classical meditations that devote themselves to the simple question: "Who am I?" We can go through our lives carrying within us an array of assumptions and images about who we are. We relate to the world from the perspective of these images and conclusions. As we begin to explore our sense of "self" we also begin to see that it is essentially formed by whatever we identify with—our bodies, thoughts, emotions, opinions, and experience. We are prone to describe ourselves by all that we identify with in the moment, saying or believing, "I am sad/happy/a failure/loveable/unworthy/etc." Many of these descriptions have a long history that becomes increasingly solid over time.

Just as we are prone to freeze our sense of "self" within the confines of these assumptions, so we tend to enact a similar process with others, identifying them by their bodies, minds, opinions, and appearances. We can feel ourselves to be just one "self" living in a world of many "selves" that we compete with, compare ourselves to, fear, envy, or love. There is a deep anxiety underlying many of these assumptions and images—the anxiety of feeling separate and apart from the world.

Our images of our "self" can deeply debilitate us, hindering creativity, growth, and our capacity to explore new horizons in our hearts and lives. With investigation we begin to see the sorrow and turmoil that follow in the wake of our identification with these images. Vast amounts of time and energy are expended in protecting, asserting, and proving ourselves or defending ourselves from threat. The divide between "self" and "other" is too often charged with mistrust and fear.

Openness of heart and depth of understanding are found through questioning the solidity of all of our images and assumptions about "self" and "other." With awareness we begin to understand that all of our notions about "I" and "you" are perhaps not so solid and immutable as they first appear to be. Our sense of who we are undergoes countless changes within a single day. The "I" that was so downcast at breakfast can be exhilarated by lunch; the "self" that glories in the success of achievement looks very different from the "self" that feels despondent in the face of failure.

Each time we hold on to or identify with any of the changing appearances of "self," we are inviting into our hearts the possibility of struggle and sorrow. Each time we are able to question and investigate those changing appearances we sow the seeds of inner balance and wisdom. There is a profound freedom in not holding any appearance to be the absolute truth of who we are.

Meditation is not concerned with cultivating a more "perfect self," improving "self," or arriving at a final conclusion of who we are. It is concerned with liberating our hearts and minds from the confines and limitations born of identification and holding. In meditation we learn to bring a gentle and inquiring attention to all the changing faces of "self" as they appear and fade away in our day. Moment to moment, we learn to question and to let go. Inviting the question "Who am I?" into our lives and hearts, we learn the art of inner freedom.

GUIDED MEDITATION: WHO AM I?

As you begin your meditation, settle into a posture of calm balance and allow your body to relax and be still.

Gently close your eyes and for a few moments bring your attention to your breathing to steady and calm your mind.

When you feel sufficiently calm and balanced inwardly, turn your attention to the thoughts, concepts, and images that arise, linger, and pass in your mind. Sense how many of those thoughts carry in subtle or glaring words the sense of "I" —"I want," "I like," "I need," "I am."

Don't judge any of those thoughts or images, simply sense the way that the sense of "I" attaches itself to them. Be aware of tendency to build a sense of "self" around a passing thought or image.

Sense the way that a kind and investigating attention brought directly to any of those thoughts or images loosens the glue of the identification.

Notice when particularly compelling thoughts, memories, or images arise how an equally strong sense of "self" appears with them and becomes defined by whatever has been taken hold of in the mind.

Sense whether it is possible to see a thought as a thought and an image as an image, and not as an absolute description of yourself.

If you sense the phrase "I am" appearing in relationship to any of those thoughts, turn the words around and ask yourself, "Am I?"

Notice when there are strong emotions present in your mind and heart, feelings of anger, fear, anxiety, or resentment.

Sense in those moments how strongly the sense of "I" appears, how you define yourself by the emotion. Again, in the face of "I am," ask yourself, "Am I?"

Notice when your attention is drawn to a sensation in your body that may be painful or even slightly uncomfortable.

Again sense the tendency to identify with that sensation—"my knee," "my back," "I am in pain" —and be aware of the fear or agitation that is born with the identification.

Explore the possibility of probing beneath the concepts and seeing a sensation as a sensation rather than as a personal description.

Sense how the sense of "I" never stands alone but is defined by whatever it is identified with. Sense how the identification solidifies everything we take hold of.

Bring a willingness to question all of the descriptions and images. Be aware of how learning to question, investigate, and let go frees our hearts and minds from the confines of all the descriptions. Thoughts, feelings, and the sensations in our body will continue to appear, yet they will also pass with greater ease.

Cultivate the willingness to question "Who am I?" in the face of everything that appears in your inner world, moment to moment.

When you are ready, open your eyes and come out of the posture.

A Mind of Stillness

As our capacity to be attentive deepens, our minds and bodies calm. Stillness becomes increasingly accessible to us and we discover a mind that can be as limitless and vast as the sky. The attention and clarity we have cultivated within our meditation practice begin to bear fruit. Stillness and openness, we come to understand, do not rely upon the absence of anything—they are revealed both in the presence and the absence of thoughts and images. The activities of our minds, when not compelled or governed by agitation or anxiety, are not obstacles to inner spaciousness and peace. The stillness and spaciousness we discover within ourselves are the source of profound happiness and unshakable balance.

The inner stillness that renews us and inspires us is not a distant goal to be striven or fought for. It is the nature of our minds. It may be no further away from us than our breath and body. We can discover it in the release of holding and agitation. In that stillness we can learn to receive the world, befriending everything that comes to us. Stillness is the source of creativity and intuitive and transforming insight. It lies at the heart of all meditative paths and disciplines.

GUIDED MEDITATION:
A MIND OF STILLNESS

Find a posture that is both deeply relaxed and alert. Let your body rest in the posture and your breathing find a natural, unforced rhythm.

Close your eyes and sense the stillness of your body in the posture. Rest in that stillness.

As you are aware of your breath moving in your body, notice the brief pause between the ending of one breath and the beginning of the next breath. Let yourself rest fully in that pause, aware of the stillness of your body and breathing.

Bring your attention just to listening. Notice the sounds that are near and far, notice the arising and passing of sound.

Sense the stillness that lies between the sounds. Let yourself rest in that stillness, listening to silence.

Sense the ways in which the sounds arise from that ground of stillness and fade away into it.

As you listen, imagine your mind to be an unclouded sky—clear, bright, and vast. Sense your mind as a space without boundaries—open and limitless.

As you rest in this sense of stillness and vastness, sense the thoughts and images that may appear as clouds in the sky.

Be aware of how those thoughts and images appear, live for a time and fade away.

Do not struggle with or resist any of the thoughts or images that arise. Simply sense the boundless capacity of your mind to embrace everything that appears without being disturbed.

Sense how everything arises and is held within the spaciousness of your mind—sounds, bodily sensations, feelings...

Let them all appear without holding on to anything. Sense them all fade away.

Let all of the seeing, feeling, hearing, sensing of this moment be held with spaciousness and openness.

Let the stillness and spaciousness of your mind pervade everything that arises.

Rest in spaciousness.

Feel deeply at home with stillness.

When you are ready, open your eyes and come out of the posture.

CHAPTER 5

A Meditative Life

M ahatma Gandhi encouraged us to "be the change we want to see in the world." Meditation would be of limited value if it were an activity explored solely within the confines of a particular posture and time frame. Instead it is intended to awaken us and enable us to live with greater sensitivity, balance, and wisdom in every dimension and moment of our lives. We can learn to live in a meditative way, embracing the complexity of our world with simplicity and calm, attending to the multiplicity of events and impressions that we meet on a daily basis with sensitivity, under-standing, and compassion.

In each moment of our lives we engage with the world. None of us has the power to exempt ourselves from that engagement. Through meditation practice we increasingly discover that we have the freedom to choose how we engage with the world, inwardly and outwardly. Mindful attention, receptive listening and wise responsiveness are the moment-to-moment applications of medi-tation that free us from anxiety, agitation, and turmoil.

Each moment of our lives brings an array of sights, sounds, touch, taste and feelings, and the world of our responses, thoughts and feelings. It is easy to be lost in that world, feel overwhelmed, or find ourselves repeating familiar patterns of reactivity and habit that undermine our well-being. But if we learn to be wholeheartedly present in each moment of our lives, we discover that agitation, confusion, and reactivity are not life sentences. We begin to see more and more clearly that the times of greatest turmoil and struggle in our lives are the times when we are most unconscious and unaware. Meditation teaches us to bring awareness and wakefulness into those moments of unconsciousness and to release the world of struggle. We discover the possibility of discovering calm in the midst of turmoil, peace in the midst of conflict, and understanding in the midst of confusion.

Meditation is not a device to make life go away or a dismissal of anything in our inner or outer world. Through meditation we learn to meet our world fully and to be a conscious participant in creating the kind of world we live in. Meditation is a path and a way of seeing that teaches us to live with a fullness of sensitivity, clarity, and responsiveness. Cultivating a meditative spirit in each moment of our lives, we come to understand that our life is the classroom in which we learn the transforming lessons of integrity, wisdom, and compassion.

Historically, a dedicated spiritual life was seen to be the domain of the monastics and hermits who had detached themselves from responsibility and engagement with life. The last decades have seen a radical shift in this paradigm. A new generation of meditation practitioners find themselves exploring ways to live a committed and vital spiritual life in the midst of families, work, and responsibility.

There is no historical blueprint or map that offers a set of formulas or prescriptions to instruct us in the ways of meeting an increasingly conflicted and complex world with ease and simplicity. There is, however, an ancient and timeless body of wisdom from all the great spiritual traditions that we draw upon and are guided by. All of the profound spiritual teachers and traditions hold at their heart the encouragement to find an inner sanctuary of balance, compassion, and wisdom founded upon inquiry and direct experience.

Inner change and transformation are not the end of the spiritual story; the second and equally significant part of that story is learning to embody the peace, understanding, and compassion we discover in every dimension and moment of our lives. Living in a meditative way, we are asked to turn peace, compassion, wisdom, clarity, and sensitivity from nouns into verbs.

What does it mean to have these qualities permeate all of our choices, actions, words, thoughts, and relationships? What does it mean to live a meditative life? A meditative life is a life where we learn to speak, act, and engage compassionately, to respond to the multiplicity of demands with simplicity and mindfulness, and to be present wholeheartedly in each moment. We learn to explore ways of ending sorrow and confusion and cultivating balance and freedom in every circumstance and moment. We see that every moment and encounter is worthy of our wholehearted attention, because it is this wise attention that reveals to us what we are asked to nurture and what we are asked to let go of to discover the peace and freedom we long for.

A meditative life begins in the life we are living. It does not depend upon having a perfect lifestyle, an absence of challenge, or reaching a point where the world no longer demands our engagement. We can learn to bring to a life of challenge, imperfection, and demand a heart and mind deeply rooted in integrity, awareness, and compassion.

Meditation practice teaches us to care wholeheartedly for the moment we are in, acknowledging that this moment is the parent of all the moments that follow. Confusion, agitation, anger, or estrangement unattended to in this moment become the history carried into the next moment. So as we learn the ways to cultivate simplicity, sensitivity, and serenity in the midst of moments of confusion, conflict, or harshness, these qualities too are borne with us into the next moments we enter.

Meditation is a journey that asks for remarkable patience and generosity. There are countless moments when we will find ourselves lost in the familiar territory of confusion, forgetfulness, or habit. Each moment of being lost is equally an invitation to begin again, to return to the present without judgment or blame, and to discover once more what it is to open, to be present and to be connected with where we are. The only place and time we can cultivate a meditative spirit is the moment we are living.

Sustained and regular formal meditation practice is an integral part of every spiritual journey. These are the times that nurture and inspire us. Yet all of us reach the moment when we open our eyes, get up from the cushion, and enter the world. This moment is not the end of our meditation practice. The spiritual stories of the great sages and teachers did not end with an enlightened experience beneath a bodhi tree, in a desert, or on a mountain top. Each one of these people re-entered the world with a commitment to embodying and deepening their understanding and compassion. This too is our challenge.

It is not difficult to be peaceful when we are undisturbed, to be compassionate when faced with the sorrow of those we love. But a meditative life asks us to find the ways of peace in the midst of challenge and to discover an unconditional compassion that embraces even those we resist most strongly. Calmness comes easily to us when life conforms to our desires and expectations, as does generosity when our lives are filled with abundance. Living with a meditative spirit asks us to find calmness and generosity in the midst of disappointment and frustration, and to live with a generous heart that can respond to need wherever it is found.

A meditative life is much vaster than a life punctuated by periods of formal meditation practice. It is a life of investigation where we carefully attend to all the moments of struggle and sorrow we meet, inwardly and outwardly. These are the moments we are asked to meet with an open heart and an inquiring spirit. These are the moments that ask for the application of understanding and compassion to find the ways of healing and the end of sorrow. Rather than resigning ourselves to the impossible, a meditative life asks us to seek for what is possible in each moment of estrangement, confusion, and conflict.

A meditative life is one lived with an awakened heart and mind that understand what it means to be fully present in each moment. We recognize that the past cannot be recovered or altered and the future lives only in our thoughts. Transformation can only happen in the present. Our lives can be filled with too many lost moments—moments that are lost in habit, unconsciousness, dwelling in the past, or endeavoring to live a future that has yet to arrive. Learning to be aware, mindful, and present in the moment we are living, we learn to reclaim those lost moments. Our lives become richer, calmer, more authentic, and meaningful. A meditative life is a life of respecting and approaching each moment with a willingness to learn the lessons of peace, connectedness, and compassion.

A Generous Heart

Generosity lies at the heart of spiritual practice. Extending generosity to ourselves and others gladdens our heart, is a direct way of healing division, and brings joy.

Generosity may have a visible expression through service, material generosity, and the myriad of ways we freely offer our time, attention, and care to another person. There is a less visible but equally powerful dimension of generosity that is a generosity of spirit. Listening to another person fully and offering forgiveness, tolerance, and acceptance are all facets of a generous heart that play a powerful role in healing anger, alienation, and fear. We cultivate this same generosity of spirit in relationship to ourselves in learning to release many of the powerful demands and expectations that wound our hearts. Inner acceptance, patience, and listening are all expressions of a generous spirit.

Generosity is essentially a way of learning to let go and live more freely and fully in our lives. We are prone to hoard, protect, defend, and accumulate. If we reflect honestly upon the consequences of these inclinations, we see clearly that they do not lead to a greater happiness, sense of abundance, or openness. Instead they breed contractedness, fear, and selfishness—essentially, they make us unhappy.

Living with a generous spirit does not imply that we are obliged to dispossess ourselves of everything in our life, nor is it an invitation to judge and condemn ourselves. The first step to living with a more generous spirit is to turn our attention to all the places and moments in our lives where feelings of deprivation or fear lead us to contract and close down and endeavor to armor ourselves with all that we accumulate.

Throughout our lives we have all been the recipients of the generosity of other people, expressed through their care and attention. Whenever we have been listened to fully, received with sensitivity and acceptance, or forgiven by another, we have experienced directly the effects of generosity. In the light of that generosity we learn to trust, open, and love.

We can all find ways of being more generous in our lives. We may not have a great deal materially to give, yet we all have the power to be profoundly generous with our attention, loving kindness, and sensitivity. Serving another person food before ourselves, helping someone across a road, taking the time to give directions to someone who is lost, or truly being willing to listen to someone who is in distress are all acts of generosity that open our own hearts and bring ease. It is not heroic actions that define generosity, but the simple willingness to give and care. Authentic generosity is always an expression of love and care, and the repercussions of generosity are a greater sense of intimacy and happiness.

A DAILY PRACTICE:
A GENEROUS HEART

Experiment with bringing into your day and life the intention to extend a generosity of spirit to others and to yourself. Sense if it is possible for you to bring loving kindness in the face of judgment, forgiveness in the face of condemnation, and attention in the moments when you are tempted to banish someone from your attention and heart.

Notice the moments in your day when you feel you don't "have enough" time, energy, or attention to truly listen or attend to someone who asks you to be present for them. Sense whether it is possible to step out of your feelings of haste and busyness and truly be present for the person before you. Sense the possibility of putting aside your own timetables and busyness to bring a wholehearted attention to those moments.

In the moments when your mind feels too full to truly listen to another person, explore the possibility of being able to step out of the swirl of your own thoughts to attend with care and sensitivity to the person asking for your attention and presence.

Sense what happens in you when someone asks you for help or a person on the street asks you for money. Generosity does not demand giving, but it does ask us to be aware of what happens within us when we are asked to give.

Notice the moments when you find yourself caught in judgment, greed, or impatience in your day. Sense what happens when instead of acting on those impulses you are able to pause and be more generous with your patience and acceptance.

Sense what happens in your own heart and mind in the moments when you find yourself able to be truly generous. Be aware of the happiness and joy that are intrinsic to authentic generosity.

Beginnings and Endings

Each day of our life is composed of countless beginnings and endings. They often pass unnoticed, the transitions blurred. Our days can appear as an uninterrupted continuum of events, activities, and talks that exhaust us. When we do not mark or notice the transitions from one activity to another we are prone to carry the unfinished business of an event or encounter that has already ended with us into the next moment, marring our capacity to attend to the moment freshly and wholeheartedly.

All too often we end a conversation feeling there is much left unsaid or regretting what we did say. Carrying those thoughts and feelings, we enter into a new contact with another person with a half-hearted attention or a heart and mind that are in reality occupied with what has already gone by. A new demand asks for our attention, often meaning that we leave the work we were doing unfinished. Preoccupied with what we were previously engaged with or resenting this new call on our attention, we approach it with reluctance or anxiety. Our plans are interrupted, our routines disrupted, or our carefully planned agendas frustrated countless times in our lives. We are asked to respond to the unexpected, to let go of our expectations, and to embrace the unanticipated.

This is the nature of all of our lives, yet a reality we frequently resist. Our resistance often means our attention is ambivalent, divided, or resentful. The source of conflict and confusion is not beginnings, endings or change, but our unwillingness to let go of what has already gone by and be present wholeheartedly with whatever each moment brings to us.

For many people there is little parity between the number of impressions, thoughts, contacts, and events they absorb and carry each day and the number that they find themselves able to let go of. When this parity is absent, our minds, hearts, and bodies carry the distress of being overburdened.

Learning to pay careful attention to the beginnings and endings in our day is in truth a way of learning to let go, to release complexity, and to find a greater simplicity and calm within our hearts, minds, and lives. It is a direct way of learning to be more present, awake, and wholehearted in life. We are learning to let go of the burden of accumulations and to calm the agitation of mind born of carrying more than we need carry. Cultivating a greater inner spaciousness, we find that our capacity to embrace the countless demands upon our attention is enhanced and our responsiveness authentic.

A DAILY PRACTICE:
BEGINNINGS AND ENDINGS

As you go into your day, take with you the conscious intention to be mindful of the beginnings and endings that are an integral part of your engagement with the world. Notice how these beginnings and endings are a part of the fabric of your day from the moment you wake in the morning.

Bring sensitive attention to the simple tasks that are a part of your day's start. Explore how possible it is to be mindful of the beginnings and endings of dressing, brushing your teeth, eating.

If you notice your attention beginning to divorce itself from where you are and what you are engaged in, explore how simple it may be just to come back and to attend fully to this moment.

As you move into your day, continue to notice the beginnings and endings that are part of your day—the beginning of a journey, the moment you arrive at your destination, the beginnings and endings of a telephone contact, a conversation, a meal, an errand in a store, driving your car, reading a paper, listening to something on the television or radio.

With each ending sense if it is possible to pause for a moment to breathe out and release what has already gone by.

As you do this, notice the quality of the attention you are able to bring to the beginning of the next contact or activity you begin.

Sense what it feels like to be wholeheartedly attentive just where you are, not leaning back into the past or forward into the future.

As you continue to explore beginnings and endings in your day, also experiment with bringing that intention to your inner world. Sense if it is possible to notice the beginnings and endings of planning, rehearsing, daydreaming, remembering—all the different streams of thought and feeling that live within us.

Initially, you might find yourself primarily aware of endings. You "wake up" from a fantasy, elaborate planning, or obsessive thinking, perhaps not even aware of how long you have been immersed in those thought patterns. In those moments of "waking up," let go of any judgment, breathe out, and bring your attention to where and how you are. This too is a beginning, the beginning of being aware.

As far as possible, sustain your commitment to being aware of the beginnings and endings that punctuate the day. Explore how far it may be possible to release what has gone by and to be fully present in all of the transitions, inwardly and outwardly, that are part of your day and your mind.

Sense the simplicity and ease that may be available to you.

Being Present: The Pull of Past and Future

Every great spiritual path suggests that our capacity to live an awakened life begins with our willingness to be present.

Learning to be present, to attend to each moment of our lives with wholehearted attention and sensitivity, is not a denial of past and future. Thoughts of past and future will continue to be part of the fabric of our lives, and in themselves they are no obstacle to being fully present right where we are. But in essence, being present means not being lost in thought or preoccupation. Lost in thoughts of the past, we become lost in guilt, regret, the world of "if only." Lost in thoughts of the future, we often surrender to anxiety and all of the planning and rehearsing born of that anxiety. To live authentically, to see and hear anything at all in this world fully, we need to be present. To love deeply and to be able to receive the world with an open heart we are asked to be present. To understand ourselves and to release the layers of confusion that burden us we need to be know what it means to be present. Our capacity for intimacy, with others and with ourselves, is interwoven with our ability to respond with an open heart and clear mind to the moment we are living.

Learning to enter each moment with a mind unclouded by preoccupation and complexity allows the richness of each moment to be revealed to us. Being present, we learn to cultivate a "beginner's mind," able to receive everything and everyone that comes into our world free of the distortions of images, judgments, and comparisons. We learn to see anew, to touch the ground, to see and hear as if for the first time. Sensitive attention enables us to be touched and be taught by all that appears in the moment.

The weight of the past and the pull of the future easily entangle us in complexity and agitation. Learning to be present is simply learning to disentangle. In letting go of our tendency to be preoccupied and lost we discover the past can be healed and the future can be entered into without anxiety.

There is a great art in learning to be present in our lives. A little attention makes all the difference. But the willingness to let go of preoccupation brings a deep spaciousness, and the commitment to take our place in each moment allows a profound sense of ease to pervade our hearts and minds.

A Daily Practice:
Being Present

As you go into your day, take with you the intention to notice the moments when your attention departs from the present to become lost thoughts of the past or future.

Some of those thoughts may be fleeting—random memories or brief psychological visits to forthcoming events or connections. Those thoughts arise and pass quickly and you find it simple to return to the moment you are in.

At other times you may find that the thoughts of past and future seem more weighted and you find yourself drawn into them. You may find yourself replaying a conversation or event that has ended in time but continued through thought.

You might find yourself drawn into thoughts about an engagement or event that has yet to arrive, rehearsing how you will engage, reflecting on what results you want to see happen, or mentally preparing your responses.

In the thoughts about the past, notice how repetitive they may be, the same story being replayed over and over.

In the thoughts about the future, again notice how few new thoughts appear in your rehearsals.

If possible, sense the emotional charge that lies beneath the thinking patterns. There may be anger, regret, or sadness permeating the thoughts of the past. There may be anxiety, fear, or expectation underlying the thoughts of the future.

In the moments when it is possible for you to sense this movement into past and future, bring your attention to your body. See if it is possible for you to find the emotional charge of the thoughts registering there. They may be impacting upon your breathing or your posture, or bringing contraction and tension into your abdomen, shoulders, or face.

Sense whether it is possible to take your attention from its immersion in the thought processes and bring it into your body.

Consciously soften any part of your body that is registering tightness or contraction.

Take a few moments to sense the touch of your feet on the ground, the air on your face, to be aware of your whole body.

In the moments when your attention is entangled in charged thought patterns about past and future, sense what happens to your relationship to the present moment. Notice how the sights, sounds, smells and feelings that are equally part of your moment have faded from awareness, becoming only a backdrop to the agitation of the thoughts.

Sense whether it is possible to reconnect with all of those sights, sounds and feelings, bringing to them a conscious attention and sensitivity.

As you feel yourself more connected to and grounded in this moment, experiment with consciously inviting into your awareness the thoughts of past and future that previously felt overwhelming.

Be aware if it is possible to hold those thoughts in your attention without the emotional charge of anxiety, sadness, regret, or expectation.

Sense the difference between being an unconscious captive of thoughts of past and future and being consciously engaged, able to think and reflect clearly.

Notice how the thoughts of past and future, when released from anxiety, arise and pass like all other thoughts, sounds, sensations, and sights.

> Sense your capacity to be fully present, not denying past or future but equally not being lost in them.
>
> Be aware of the calmness and balance born of being fully present one moment at a time.

Challenging Habit: Awakening our Lives

An awakened life is one in which the confines of habit are challenged through interest and attention. Habit and wakefulness are rarely compatible. Habit leads us to see life through the eyes of images and assumptions. Awareness teaches us to see each moment, event, person and ourselves anew. Habit binds us to the past, awareness awakens us to the present. Habit distances us from the moment-to-moment realities of our life. Awareness is the cultivation of intimacy within each moment. Habit inclines us to dismiss many of the simple activities and events of our day as being insignificant or unworthy. Awareness is free of hierarchies of value, deeming every single moment and activity of our day as being worthy of our wholehearted attention.

In all of the moments of our lives that are governed by habit we live only on the surface of existence, disconnected from its depth and richness. Lost in habit, we deny ourselves the capacity to approach each moment with a beginner's mind, the capacity to see anew and to be taught by life.

Awareness dissolves habit and gives birth to openness and a deepening connection with all life. It teaches us to probe beneath the surface of all things—our conclusions, opinions, images, and assumptions—to take nothing for granted in this life. Rather than believing we "know" someone, ourselves, or all that we can learn

149

from any moment in life, awareness teaches us to rest in a deeper "not knowing" and questioning. This is the home of wonder, learning, and mystery.

Habit appears to relieve us of the need to be present, enabling us to attend to multiple tasks at the same time. We can wash the dishes while rehearsing our day. We can appear to listen to another while planning our next encounter. We can walk while entertaining our favorite fantasy. Habit equally appears to relieve us of the need to deepen our understanding of ourselves or of another person. If we conclude someone is boring, irritating, or obnoxious and freeze them into that assumption, we may feel no need to probe our own reactivity nor seek to find a greater tolerance, acceptance, or patience within ourselves. If we hold an image of ourselves as being a failure, inadequate, or always right in our opinions, we may also feel no urgency to probe our own conclusions and self-images and find inner transformation.

Habit disconnects us from the moment-to-moment realities of our lives and leads us to live in a world created by our thoughts and images. Awareness connects us, seeking to discover the possibilities of each moment. With awareness and wisdom we come to understand that none of our images can ever describe the truth of ourselves, another person or anything we meet in our life.

Habit engenders dullness and sensitivity, and awareness engenders vitality and depth. In search of peace, completeness, and understanding we increasingly treasure vitality and depth, and learn to gently probe the areas of our lives, inwardly and outwardly, that are dulled by habit.

A DAILY PRACTICE:
CHALLENGING HABIT: AWAKENING OUR LIVES

Reflect upon your life and all of the activities you frequently engage in, sensing where habit is most strongly present.

You might see habit being the governing force in some of the simple actions you undertake—how you wash your dishes, cook a meal, drive your car or walk to work.

You might see that it is within the repetitive activities that are part of all of our lives that we are most prone to becoming habitual and mechanical.

Take just one or two activities and commit yourself to undertaking them as if for the first time.

As you wash your dishes, sense all of the sensations and movements involved—the touch of the water on your skin, your hand touching a glass, the movement of your arm. Have the intention of bringing a genuine depth of sensitivity to that moment.

If there is a familiar path you walk many times in your life—up a flight of stairs, to your bus stop or into your workplace—experiment with walking that path with a fullness of sensitivity and a commitment to being present in each step.

Sense if there are people in your life who have in some way been dismissed from your heart because of an image or assumption you hold about them. They may be the people you find yourself avoiding, the person in your neighborhood store who is hardly seen through lack of interest, or someone who has in some way offended you. Make a commitment to meeting that person, seeing and listening to them with a fullness of sensitivity and attention, as if they were your dearest friend or as if this was both the first and last time you would ever have the opportunity to know that person. Sense what happens when you are willing to probe beneath your images and conclusions.

Each day make a simple commitment to bring a fullness of sensitivity and interest to just one area of your life that you sense is governed by habit.

Sense how the commitment to awareness has the power to dissolve habit in a moment, allowing a new depth and sensitivity to emerge.

Eating

Our life and well-being rely upon the nourishment we receive. Every mouthful of food we eat is the result of the efforts of the numerous people involved in its growth and the benevolence of nature. For the countless people in our world who face daily deprivation, every meal is a blessing and a lifeline to survival. For those of us who live with greater abundance and security, food is often taken for granted or has assumed layers of emotional overtone.

Moments of mindful eating may be rare in our lives. When we are rushed, food is consumed in haste, something used solely to subdue the distraction of our body's hunger. When our minds are overly full of preoccupation, meals are often eaten habitually, something to get over so we can resume the obsessive thinking we are more interested in. When we are bored, food can become a primary means of distraction. In the midst of distress, food is frequently turned to as a source of comfort. Food can become a substitute for the seemingly impossible task of understanding the source of inner turmoil.

Learning to approach eating with care and sensitivity is a direct way of cultivating appreciation and nurturing moments of calm in our days. Approaching meals with intentional awareness cultivates a deeper sense of connection with all life and an appreciation of how precious is our well-being. Learning to stop when we eat, to be fully attentive, is a powerful way of introducing moments of stillness and calm into our day.

It can be helpful to approach at least one meal a day with the intention of focusing fully upon it, sitting down to eat and consciously unhooking from telephones, television or reading. Approach this as a time of letting go of haste and busyness. Many people find it useful to have one meal a day in silence, allowing their minds and bodies a time of renewal and ease.

GUIDED MEDITATION:
EATING

As you sit down with your food, take a few moments just to consciously relax your body and sit quietly for a moment or two.

Sense the space around you, listen to the sounds around you, feel the contact of your body with the chair and the touch of your feet on the ground.

Calmly pass your eyes over the food on your plate.

Sense the different textures, shapes, smells, and colors of the food.

As you move to pick up your fork or spoon, be present within the movement of your arms and hands. Sense the sensation of your hand taking hold of your cutlery.

As you put the food in your mouth, notice the taste as the food contacts your taste buds.

Chew mindfully, savoring the taste of the food.

Notice the moments when your mind is already focused on the next bite, and gently bring your attention back to savor the food you are eating now. You might even experiment with putting your spoon or fork down after each mouthful.

As you swallow and move to take up the next mouthful of food, stay clearly present with that movement.

Let the meal from beginning to ending be a time of appreciation and sensitivity.

Notice the changing sensations in your body as they shift from hunger to satisfaction.

Let the whole time of your meal be a dedicated time of calmness and mindfulness.

Sense within your body when you have eaten enough and stop at that point.

As you end your meal, again bring your attention into your body, sensing its ease.

Again, before getting up, feel the contact of your body on the chair, your feet touching the ground, and the sights and sounds of that moment.

Heartfelt Communication

One of the most challenging dimensions of our lives to bring awareness into is the dimension of communication. Yet our words are powerful, holding within them the capacity to harm and to heal, to be a source of joy or sorrow. Through our speech we have the power to bridge the separations that divide us from others and find intimacy and understanding. Our words can also carry the power to create new rifts and further alienation.

Through our speech we communicate our thoughts, emotions, and states of mind. We also receive the inner landscape of others' minds and hearts through the ways in which they communicate with us. Anger, sadness and fear all find form in our words, as do appreciation, generosity, and tenderness. Learning to be increasingly mindful of our communication is a way of becoming increasingly aware of the inner climate that lies beneath the words.

There are times when we feel uncomfortable and uncertain in silence, and filling that space with words becomes a way of distancing ourselves from that discomfort. Our words become a means of finding reassurance and familiarity. There are also moments when are words are habitual and reactive. We may find ourselves uttering words of harshness and condemnation that we later regret, yet they fly from our mouths with an intensity and unconsciousness that sometimes frightens us. In the moments when we feel most governed by anxiety, agitation or anger our speech tends to be the most impulsive, at times wounding ourselves or another person. In learning to be more awake and sensitive within our speech, we can appreciate the impact it has upon our own consciousness and upon the heart of another.

Wise speech is a meditative practice. Are our words spoken in a tone and at a time when they can be truly listened to by another? Are we saying what is true and useful? What are the intentions in our speech—do we seek to harm or to heal?

Our relationships, families, communities, and world plead for greater understanding and communication. In our own lives and connections with others we can be a conscious participant in contributing to the ending of alienation and mistrust through our own commitment to mindful communication.

A Daily Practice:
Mindful Speech

As you go into your day, take with you the intention to be mindful of all the different moments of communication.

Notice how your awareness of speech is different in different contexts.

Be aware of how you speak with the people you feel somewhat neutral towards—the person in the store, the coffee shop, the ticket seller.

Take a day when you approach those people differently. Look into their eyes as you request something or thank them. In even the few words you use in these contacts, experiment with speaking in a heartfelt way, making a genuine connection with that person.

Stay in contact with your speech in the moments when your are speaking to someone you care for and feel affection for. Be aware of the words you are speaking and what they are communicating. Sense whether you are comfortable in silence.

Be aware of your speech in the moments you are in contact with someone you dislike or feel threatened by or in situations that are charged with anger or blame. In those moments, try to stay in touch with your own emotional landscape before you speak. Can your words be born of that awareness rather being purely reactive? Is it possible for you to stay connected with the person you feel angry towards or are receiving anger from rather than withdrawing and becoming lost in the anxiety or anger? Sense whether it is possible in those charged moments to speak with calmness and care or to be silent rather than uttering words that may wound.

An aid to being increasingly aware within your communication is to allow your attention to rest more fully in your throat, lips, and face. Sense what happens in those areas when you speak and before you speak.

It is important to cultivate an awareness in speaking that is free from judgment or condemnation. The right attitude is to be simply interested in exploring what happens in this powerful dimension of our lives. There may be a wisdom in cultivating restraint—in the times when we feel most compelled by anger or anxiety it can be helpful to learn to pause before speaking. Restraint is different from suppression: the primary motivation in restraint is to be aware and to understand.

As you are increasingly aware of your speech throughout your day, sense its potential to be a source of intimacy and connectedness.

Receptive Listening

Communication is a twofold process, involving not only speaking with authenticity and awareness, but also listening with a deep receptivity.

There is a great art in learning to be mindful in listening. We can learn to listen to ourselves as we speak, allowing our words to rise from an inner stillness and calm. We can also learn to bring that same receptivity and stillness to listening to others, being wholehearted in our receptivity rather than formulating our responses and impatiently waiting for a moment to interject them.

Mindful communication is more than just an exchange of words—it is a time that holds the possibility of a genuine connection and bond of intimacy with another. When we listen to another, are we listening in a non-judgmental way? Are we able to offer a patient presence that is genuinely connected with the person speaking to us?

Carrying with us into our lives the commitment to conscious communication, we learn to value the bonds we form with all those who are part of our lives. We learn to cultivate intimacy and respect.

A Daily Practice:
Receptive Listening

Bring with you into your day the commitment to listen whole-heartedly in all the moments when someone is asking for your attention and presence.

In contact with a friend, listen with awareness and spaciousness.

Listen with your heart, sensing their reaching out to forge a connection with you and be fully present.

Listen with patience, noticing the moments when with impatience or boredom you start to disconnect. See if you can bring your attention back to be fully present.

Listen with openness, instead of preparing your responses or waiting for a lull in their speech so you can say something you deem to be more interesting or important.

Notice if there are moments when you start to judge whatever they are recounting to you. Sense whether it is possible to let go of those judgments and renew your commitment to being fully present with the person in front of you.

Bring awareness into those moments in your day when you are listening to someone who is distressed or angry.

Sense what happens in your own body, mind and heart as you listen to distress or anger.

Notice how you may be prone to stop listening as you prepare your defenses or retorts. Sense if you feel hurt or helpless as you absorb the words of another.

When faced with someone who is enraged, it may be helpful to explore what it means to stay connected with that person without being lost in the barrage of their words. Are you able to sustain eye contact with them, sense the pain or frustration that underlies their anger, and listen without feeling attacked? Are you able to leave their anger with them rather than feeling you need to defend yourself or respond in kind? Listening to someone who is deeply distressed or in pain can be deeply challenging.

As you listen to someone recounting to you their heartache, notice if as a reaction to feeling helpless, you begin to search for formulas or prescriptions to 'fix' their pain. This may not be what is being asked of you. What is being asked for is a compassionate presence.

Faced with someone in distress, explore what it may mean simply to bring a compassionate, open stillness that can receive that sorrow.

Experiment with listening to yourself as you speak, sensing whether your speech is a genuine expression of care and sensitivity. Are you saying what you wish to say, communicating what you most need to communicate? Are you able to listen to your own heart and mind before the words are spoken?

Nature: A Place of Connection

The natural world is a powerful ally reminding us of the possibility of discovering richness, appreciation, and sensitivity in all the moments of our lives. Awake to the unfolding seasons, the buds and growth of spring, the abundance of summer, the fading in fall, and the dormancy of winter, we remember too the inevitable seasons of change within our own lives. Birth and death, arising and passing are the rhythms of everything in our own lives inwardly and outwardly, reminding us to receive life with a fullness of appreciation and yet also to find the ease of being able to let go in all of the endings that are part of our lives.

When our hearts and minds are burdened, overfull, or contracted, forging a connection with the natural world is a way of finding a greater simplicity and ease. Learning to see fully, to appreciate the texture and color of a single leaf, to listen wholeheartedly to the song of a bird, we remember that life is vaster than just the current contents of our minds and hearts. We sense our place in the natural rhythm of all things. When our minds feel most obsessed or preoccupied, in learning to open our eyes and hearts to the natural world around us we can discover a greater spaciousness and a sense of refuge within its simplicity.

The lessons we learn within nature are the same lessons we are asked to learn in our own lives. The daffodil does not demand to be a rose, the wilting flower does not argue with the natural rhythm of its ending. Everything arises and changes in nature according to conditions. The soil, a seed, rain, and sun combine for a flower to bloom. Everything in our life too grows from a combination of conditions that we cannot always control or govern. Control, expectation, demand, and argument destroy the ease possible for us in our lives.

Appreciation and sensitivity are integral to a life of joy and richness. None of these qualities are far away from us. Opening our eyes and hearts to the world around us in this moment, we cultivate the pathways of appreciation. Sensitive to the world around us, we are reminded to bring that same sensitivity to attending to our inner world. Learning to receive the natural world with appreciation and connectedness, we remember the possibility of receiving ourselves in the same spirit.

A DAILY PRACTICE:
NATURE: A PLACE OF CONNECTION

Experiment with taking a day of bringing a wholehearted attention to the sensory doors of seeing and listening.

When you wake in the morning, take a few moments to connect fully with the sights and sounds of your day. You may see the sun touching the ground outside your window. Look at both the ground illuminated by the light and the places of shadow. You may see the raindrops on your window. See fully their shape and movement.

Take a few moments to listen fully. Listen to the sounds of birds as they appear and fade away or the sound of the wind in the branches of the trees. Bring a total attention to just listening to the sounds of nature.

As you walk out of your house, take a few moments to pause and sense the natural world. Bring your attention to see fully a single blade of grass, a leaf on a tree, or the bare earth. Explore with your eyes all of the texture, color, and shape held within that moment. Notice the intricacy of a single leaf, holding it fully in your attention.

If you are able to walk in nature, explore the possibility of seeing and hearing fully, without expectation or preference, simply absorbing the world around you. See the birds in the sky and the spaciousness of the sky itself. Focus your attention upon a single cloud, absorbing its shape and color with your attention.

There are moments when your attention may get lost in judgment, concepts, and descriptions. Sense the possibility of coming back to just seeing and just listening, allowing all of the descriptions to be just a whisper in the mind.

Sense the deepening appreciation and sensitivity that are born of your wholehearted attention.

Sense the deepening connectedness and richness that are born of your capacity to see and listen deeply and fully.

One Thing at a Time

Inner calm and well-being are the first casualties of the frantic pace of our lives as we heroically endeavor to do more and more each day. The inner and outer pressures to produce, perform, and achieve exact a harmful toll upon inner spaciousness and balance. Increasingly we are prone to measure and evaluate our sense of worth by all that we are able to attain or produce rather than by our capacity to live fully with an open heart and clear mind. Times of stillness and of attending to the quality of our lives are dismissed as being wasted moments.

Caught in the mythology that equates worth with busyness, we begin to believe that we cannot afford to take the time to care for our hearts, minds, and bodies. In our society it is not uncommon for people to take greater care of their cars than of their hearts, minds, and bodies. The effects of this mythology are profound, as our bodies become increasingly distressed and our minds fragmented and contracted.

It is more truthful to say that we cannot afford *not* to care for the quality of our inner world. If confusion and fragmentation are our prevailing inner climate, they will manifest in every area of our lives. If inner clarity, balance, and sensitivity prevail, however, they too will pervade all of our actions, thoughts, and relationships.

Inner serenity, openness, receptivity, and sensitivity are not just fortunate accidents randomly encountered in our lives, but qualities that are consciously cultivated in the midst of all of the events and moments of our lives. The training ground of attentiveness and balance is when we face what appears to be an unending stream of demand and challenge. Here we learn to pay attention to just one thing and one moment at a time. We may produce and achieve less, yet we will also discover the possibility of living wholeheartedly with a mind and heart at peace.

A DAILY PRACTICE:
ONE THING AT A TIME

Experiment with dedicating a day to undertaking just one thing at a time with wholehearted attention.

Start in the morning from the moment that you awake. As you dress, shower and eat breakfast, explore what it means to attend fully to just one activity at a time. Sense your body moving in those activities—all the sounds, sights, tastes, smells, and sensations held within that moment.

Each time your mind begins to lean into the next moment with plans, anticipation, rehearsal, or anxiety, just gently come back to where you are.

As you move into your day, walking to your car or bus stop, sense what it means just to walk with your attention fully present within your body.

Sense what it means to let go of hurrying. Be aware that hurrying is a state of mind born of being preoccupied with arrivals and results rather than attending to the present. Doing one thing at a time does not mean everything being performed at a snail's pace. We discover we can often do things quickly and fully without hurrying.

When you engage in conversations during your day, on the telephone or directly with another person, sense what it means to listen wholeheartedly and to be fully present with that person.

If you are writing, give your attention to feeling the touch of the pen in your hand, the movement of your hand as you write.

When you stop to eat, refrain from picking up a newspaper or book and be wholeheartedly present just with the activity of eating.

Approach each task in the day with the willingness to devote an undivided attention to it.

If you find that your pace of activity begins to accelerate and you feel hurried, take that moment just to pause and be still. Be aware of your body and breathing and allow the sense of being rushed to calm.

Throughout the day, commit yourself to just attending to one thing at a time with a sensitive attention.

As you return home in the evening, sustain the dedication to being fully present. As you prepare food, talk with a friend, read, listen to music, undertake each of these things with a genuine dedication to being awake and present within them.

Sense what happens for you as you begin to integrate body, mind, heart, and present moment. Be aware of the calmness that may begin to appear, the way in which less is taken for granted, and your growing capacity to approach each moment with sensitivity and appreciation.

Notice the moments when your attention is divided or scattered and explore in those moments the possibility of pausing, being still and again renewing your intention to be fully present and balanced.

Receive all of the moments of tension, contractedness, and inner busyness as messengers inviting you to return to a greater simplicity and attentiveness in the moment.

Our Body as an Ally

All that we do, have done and will do in our life will be done within our body. Learning to be present in our body in all its movements, responses, and acts, we learn to be present in the whole of our lives.

Our bodies and minds are often divided, strangers to each other. Caught in the busyness and momentum of our thoughts, plans, and agitation, our bodies are easily neglected, becoming a casualty of our mind's overload. They are too often treated like a rented vehicle—useful for getting to our destinations, yet rarely held with respect and sensitivity.

Our bodies, their movements, acts, and gestures, can be governed by habit and reactivity. Equally they can be the home and the source of wakefulness and sensitivity. Learning to be more present in our bodies is a direct means of healing the mind—body division and calming the agitation of our thoughts. Our body can be a great ally in the cultivation of a wakeful life.

A DAILY PRACTICE:
OUR BODY AS AN ALLY

Experiment with taking a day when you commit yourself to being mindful and aware within your body.

Each hour, no matter what you are doing, take just a few moments to stop and be still.

In those moments, bring your attention to your body. Sense how your body is held, whether standing, sitting, walking, or lying down.

Throughout your day, notice which of these postures your body is in. When you stand, be fully aware of standing; when sitting, just sit; when walking, be present in each step; when lying down, sense the ease of your body.

Be aware of how you are holding your shoulders, your face and jaw, your hands. Sense whether you are carrying tension or tightness in those areas and consciously soften them moment to moment.

Be aware of the internal world of your body, your breathing, and all the different sensations that your body is manifesting.

Listen to the messages of your body—if your breath is contracted or shortened, consciously take a few deeper in-breaths and follow your out-breath to its very end.

Sense what it feels like to deeply relax your body.

Bring a gentle attention to all the places where your body connects with the ground and with a chair.

Relax into just being still for a few moments, bringing your mind into your body.

Sense what difference it makes to cultivate those mindful pauses regularly in your day, feeling at home and at ease within your body.

As you again move or act, see if it is possible to notice the moments when your mind and body separate from one another. Be aware of the times of moving towards a destination when your mind has arrived long before your body. Explore the possibility of coming back to your body.

In the more repetitive activities of your day—washing dishes, driving, preparing a meal—notice how easily your attention drifts into thought or into the endings yet to arrive.

Sense if it is possible to return to a more sensitive bodily awareness, learning to pause and to dispel the disconnection.

Whatever you are doing in your day, explore the possibility of always being able to bring your attention into your body, calming your mind through being present within the life of your body.

Let your body be an ally of awareness, constantly reminding you to be present and to live each moment fully.

Simplicity

On daily basis we face an ongoing bombardment of messages that endeavor to convince us that having more, becoming more, doing more and possessing more are the pathways to happiness, fulfillment, and security. All of the great spiritual traditions deliver a somewhat different message, suggesting that genuine happiness lies within our own hearts and minds and can never be truly secured through the multiplicity of possessions, identities, and achievements we can gather in our lives. It is also suggested that none of what we can accumulate will ever effectively armor us against the rhythms of change that will ask us to meet loss, failure, and disappointment with grace. Fulfillment will be found through the authenticity of our hearts and lives, rather than resting upon the shaky foundations of possession and accumulation.

By not pursuing or gathering more than we need for our well-being we are letting go of the pathways of greed and exaggerated need that damage our world. Learning to find well-being in simplicity is a direct way of caring for ourselves and our world.

Simplicity is a multi-dimensional exploration. Cultivating greater simplicity in our lives does not demand that we forsake our homes and families, divorce ourselves from our careers or abandon all of our possessions. Simplicity is also a direct expression and embodiment of understanding. We see that bottomless need and want are frequently driven by an inner sense of impoverishment that can never be satisfied by the multiplicity of things that we surround ourselves with. We begin to notice that the moments of desperate wanting, pursuit, and need that arise in our days are inextricably linked to an equally dire sense of anxiety. We fill our lives with distraction and busyness to divert ourselves from the painful sense of there being something amiss when we are not constantly occupied. Coming home from work, sitting on a train and in countless other situations when "doing" is not demanded of us, we are prone to immediately fill the silence and stillness with distraction.

As our minds are increasingly acclimatized to non-stop activity, sensory impressions, and distraction, it becomes increasingly difficult for us to "un-hook" and be still. We see times of simplicity and non-doing as wasted or uncomfortable moments. Thomas Merton, a great Christian mystic, described the habit of doing too much, answering to too many demands, taking on too many projects, as the most prevalent form of contemporary violence.

Meditative paths do not judge the anxiety or sense of impoverishment that may drive us, but invite us to attend to them directly rather than endeavoring to camouflage them with busyness and obsession. At the heart of every meditative path lies the commitment to caring for our well-being with respect and sensitivity. It is the training ground for learning to bring that same respect and sensitivity to every moment and encounter in our lives.

Simplicity is not the pursuit of austerity but an ongoing life exploration that asks us to carefully examine what truly contributes to well-being and what undermines inner balance, happiness, and spaciousness. We can bring the exploration of simplicity into every area of our lives—the choices we make, the actions we engage in, the goals that can obsess us, our speech, the ways we use our time, and our relationship to the world of things, possessions, opinions, and roles. In doing so, we begin to see that simplicity is not a rejection of anything, but is in reality the most compassionate way of being in this world. We learn to treasure moments of stillness, finding within them a genuine sense of ease and spaciousness.

A Daily Practice:
Simplicity

As you move into your day, take with you the intention to notice all the moments when no specific activity demands your attention. They might be moments travelling to or from work, breaks in your working day, or a lull at the end of the day in which nothing demands your engagement.

Sense what happens in your mind and body in those moments. Be aware if you are carrying an inclination to immediately fill that space with something to occupy your attention. There may be an inclination to pick up a book, turn on the radio, make a telephone call, or search for food.

See if it is possible to restrain the immediate impulse towards busyness or distraction and to simply rest in that moment.

Initially you may find that these spaces of "nothing to do" feel moderately uncomfortable or carry with them a sense of there being something missing. Bring your attention to your body and mind to simply explore the landscape of that sense of unease, without judging it in any way.

Reflect on how you might feel at home in stillness, in "non-doing."

Initially, the simplicity of stillness and "non-doing" may reveal the complexity and busyness of your mind. Pay attention to the thought streams that arise in those moments rather than being pushed by them into new cycles of busyness.

You might experiment with adopting the lulls in your day as times when you commit yourself to stillness and simplicity. They can be moments in which you befriend your mind and body, learn to let go of some of the busyness that drives you, and discover the deep sense of ease and resting in the moment that may be available to you. Instead of focusing upon what appears to be missing, bring your attention to what is present. The capacity to connect with your mind, body, and present moment is available to you.

You may discover that your capacity to feel at ease in stillness and simplicity brings with it a greater sensitivity and awareness. Let stillness and simplicity be regular companions in each day, a source of renewal and creativity.

Take some moments to reflect upon your life and sense where it is cluttered by objects that no longer serve you well. What are you holding on to, out of anxiety, that you no longer need? Sense whether letting it go would create more spaciousness in your life.

Reflect upon what your mind most frequently dwells upon.

Sense whether the spaciousness of your own mind has been undermined by preoccupations, fantasies, goals, or desires that do not contribute to your well-being. Is it possible to let them go?

Reflect on your life and sense where it may be possible for you to create a greater simplicity. What would you be asked to let go of?

Sense how many of the richest and deepest moments of happiness in your life have been moments of great simplicity.

Reflect on what it would mean for simplicity to be a dedicated theme in your life.

Simplicity in Action

Genuine simplicity does not depend upon the absence of activity or engagement. In our lives we act, make choices, and move through a world that needs our attention. The activities we engage in, when undertaken with awareness, communicate and embody all that we value and respect. Our aspirations are realized through action and expression. Our choices and acts have the power to communicate a profound calmness, compassion, integrity, and connectedness.

A meditative life does not depend upon retreating to the nearest monastery or cave, but learning to be present in all the activities of our lives with awareness and balance. The countless activities that make up our days are not obstacles to peace or stillness. Undertaken with mindfulness and sensitivity, they become the places in which we learn to deepen the calmness and peace we treasure.

The wisest people, who have been central in bringing about the greatest social, political, and spiritual transformations, have been people of engagement and action. Moved by compassion, understanding, and care, they have been fully present in their communities, relationships, and world. Their inner core of balance and understanding has found its expression in the choices and activities they have dedicated themselves to.

In a life that often seems overfull, with little ease or "non-doing," we may come to believe that we have to postpone a deep spiritual life until we reach a point where life asks less of us. Yet a meditative life doesn't demand that we forsake the world, but that we forsake postponement. We can bring simplicity and stillness to our lives in the midst of activity.

A DAILY PRACTICE:
SIMPLICITY IN ACTION

Whatever activity we engage in, from the most simple to the most complex, our bodies will be part of it. As you begin an activity, notice which part of your body is most directly engaged or in motion. If you are writing, washing dishes, or driving, it might be your hands. If you are listening to someone, it may be your ears. If you are moving, it may be your feet and legs that make that the most predominant impression.

Explore whether it is possible to root your attention in the part of your body most predominantly engaged in the activity.

Many activities are multi-dimensional, involving our bodies in different ways, so the place of predominant impression in your body may change. Let your attention move with those changes.

One of the states of mind that brings with it complexity and agitation is "hurrying." Moving quickly holds no intrinsic power to create agitation, but "hurrying" invariably leaves us feeling scattered and exhausted. Notice the moments when you begin to feel rushed or hurried. Sense those feelings as states of mind that are impacting upon your body, leading you to lean forward into a moment that hasn't arrived.

Sense whether it is possible for you to slow down a little in those moments and bring your attention back into your body.

Another of the states of mind that acts as a primary obstacle to sensitivity and wakefulness is boredom. Learn to regard boredom as a cue that you have in some way become disconnected from the moment.

Instead of reaching for distraction in moments of feeling bored, turn your attention directly towards the boredom itself. Explore it with your attention, try to find where it lives and the distance it has created between you and the simple richness of the moment.

Experiment with staying connected with your body in moments of activity. Be sensitive to the sensation in your hands, legs, or whatever part of your body is most predominantly engaged.

In many of the activities we engage in our hands play a central role. Bringing awareness back into your hands in the moments when you become lost in thought or habit is a direct way of returning to the present and to simplicity.

Experiment with bringing an intentional sensitivity to all the moments in your day when you are engaged in activity.

Notice the ways in which mindful attention, brought to the simplest of acts, allows them to be moments of simplicity and calm

Walking with Awareness

Walking is an integral part of all of our lives yet is often regarded solely as a utilitarian way of reaching the destinations we have our minds set on. Each day we walk, moving from one room to another, one place to another, up stairs, down streets, and through our communities and in nature. Times of walking invite us to be present where we are, to integrate our minds and bodies, and connect with our environment.

We perhaps see that these times of movement can also be some of the most habitual moments in our lives. Walking becomes a means to an end, a way of arriving somewhere yet to be reached. We can also learn to be fully present in those moments, not inclining towards the future but finding a calm presence and attention in each step we take. We can learn to walk in an undistracted way, resting in each step. We can learn to pull our attention back from the destinations we have yet to arrive at and find a deeper appreciation of where we are.

Many meditative traditions give as equal an emphasis to walking meditation as to formal sitting meditation. Walking meditation is a direct way of acknowledging that much of our lives is spent in movement, interfacing and interacting with the world around us. We need to embrace this dimension of our lives with awareness, not regarding it as secondary in importance to formal meditation practice.

In walking meditation we can learn to be focused in movement, our minds and bodies unified in calmness. We can discover the possibility of walking through a world of busyness, with countless sights, sounds, and impressions, without being lost in agitation. Cultivating mindfulness in walking, we reclaim the moments in our lives that are too often lost in distraction and in thoughts of the future.

Every step we take in our lives can be a gesture of calmness, feeling the ground beneath our feet and being alive and present within our bodies. Every time we walk can be a time we dedicate to sensitivity, receiving the world of impressions with simplicity and receptivity. Every step we take can be a means to being here in this moment, caring for the quality of our hearts and minds. We can learn to walk through a world of busyness with poise and balance.

A DAILY PRACTICE:
WALKING WITH AWARENESS

As you go into your day, take with you the intention to be aware of your body in all the moments when you are walking.

Try to notice the moments when your body begins to move. When you stand up, remind yourself to be aware of yourself standing.

If possible take just a moment to stand still, sensing the contact of your feet with the ground and the uprightness of your posture.

Sense if your attention has already leapt ahead to the destination you intend to move towards.

Bring your attention back to your body, letting go of the plans or the thoughts about your arrival.

As you begin to move, experiment with keeping your attention firmly but gently anchored within your body.

Be as present as you are able to be within each step, aware of the different sights and sounds that come to you yet not becoming lost in them.

Sense your feet lifting, your legs moving, the weight of your body shifting with each step.

Notice that if you are able to slow down your pace even slightly, your walking is no longer governed by habit but is held within awareness.

Sense when your walking is compelled by hurrying or agitation and notice that those states of mind exile you from your body.

Explore the ways that you may be able to let go of the haste, connect with your body, and be present in each of the steps you take,

When you arrive at your destination, if possible take a moment to stand still once more, feeling your feet and your connection with the earth.

FORMAL WALKING MEDITATION

It may be possible for you to find a few moments in your day to explore walking meditation in a more formal way.

Find a path for yourself, inside or outside, to walk on. It need not be a particularly long path—15 or 20 yards is ample.

Start your walking meditation by taking a few moments to stand still and gently close your eyes.

Feel the touch of your feet on the ground, the air on your skin. Be aware of the sounds around you and the variety of sensations within your body.

Let yourself relax in the standing posture and then open your eyes, focusing your attention on the ground just in front of you

Establish a pace of walking that is just a little slower than your usual walking rhythm.

As you lift your foot to take your first step, be aware of all of the sensations that occur in your foot and leg in that process of lifting.

Feel your foot move through the air and the sensations that arise as your foot once more touches the ground.

Sense which part of your foot first makes contact with the ground and be present with attention in the completion of the step.

Be aware of the shift in your body weight as you begin to take the next step.

If your attention is drawn into thought, just notice it and gently return to be aware of your body as wholeheartedly as possible.

Continue to walk on your path, resting in each step, cultivating calmness and wholehearted attention.

When you reach the end of your walking path, again just stand still for a moment or two, resting in your body and then begin to turn to retrace your steps.

Each time your attention drifts away from your body, sense the possibility of letting go of the distractedness and once more returning to be aware of the simple process of walking.

When you walk, just walk without thought of destination or arrival.

As your attention deepens you may find that the pace of your walking slows down even more. Find a pace that is unforced and comfortable.

Experiment with the walking meditation whenever possible in your day. Sense the calmness and ease born of the unification of mind, body, and present moment.

Conclusion

Through dedicated times of meditation we deepen not only our capacity to find inner spaciousness and balance, but also our confidence in our capacity to realize the compassion and depth we aspire to in our lives. The calmness and stillness we begin to discover within ourselves enrich not only our own well-being but also the well-being of our world.

The keys to deepening meditation are patience and commitment. No one's meditation practice is linear or predictable. Times of great calmness and depth may be followed by storms of thought or waves of agitation. The calmness and agitation both invite our attention and presence. Steady perseverance allows us to learn from both the highs and lows that appear in our practice. Increasingly we learn to be awake, present, and compassionate in all the joys and sorrows, the moments of ease and the moments of challenge. We begin to discover within ourselves a genuine peace born of befriending all things. Our hearts and minds are transformed by awareness and understanding. Our lives and relationships are transformed by compassion and loving kindness.

Life will continue to bring us countless moments that ask for our compassion, times of conflict that ask for healing, and moments of confusion that plead for peace. Meditation teaches us a wise responsiveness and a way of being present in our life that is authentic and rich. We cultivate on a moment-to-moment level a heart and mind that are receptive to understanding, inclined to compassion, and dedicated to peace.

The right moment to begin to meditate is the moment we are in, in the midst of the life we are living. The dedication we bring to cultivating a meditative life will bear fruit in the deepening serenity and responsiveness we discover. An awakened heart and a mind of calmness and clarity are priceless treasures.